The D
GENERATION

Bumper Book of Aussie Hero's

*"Lives of great men all remind us
We can make our lives sublime
And, departing, leave behind us
Footprints on the sands of time"*

(Longfellow, <u>A Psalm of Life</u>, 1855).

"May I have a window seat please?"

R. Trimbole, <u>Final words</u>, 1984

<u>ERRATUM:</u> following a decree of the Australian Metric Board, would readers please note than on page 75 the character referred to as "Lady Chatterley" now receives "a good 18.42 centimetres".

<u>N.B.</u> The symbol  next to any hero indicates that they are yet to be made the subject of an Australian feature film or mini-series.

WRITTEN BY

Santo Cilauro

Thomas Gleisner

Robert Sitch

*Our sincerest thanks must go to Andrew Knight and John Alsop
who laboured ceaselessly to bring a sophisticated, European
wit to the project, spending many hours on all the best jokes,
including a month on this paragraph alone.*

ILLUSTRATIONS

Linda Cerkvenik

Sam Morel

Megan Power

Patricia Stewart

Cathy van Ee

PHOTOGRAPHS

Rob Blackburn

Nick Tapp

ABC Publicity (!)

ADDITIONAL MATERIAL

Magda Szubanski

The D GENERATION

Bumper Book of Aussie Hero's

PENGUIN BOOKS

For Ferdinand Marcos.

Penguin Books Australia Ltd,
487 Maroondah Highway, P.O. Box 257
Ringwood, Victoria, 3134, Australia
Penguin Books Ltd,
Harmondsworth, Middlesex, England
40 West 23rd Street, New York, N.Y. 10010. U.S.A.
Penguin Books Canada Limited,
2801 John Street, Markham, Ontario, Canada L3R 1B4
Penguin Books (N.Z.) Ltd,
182-190 Wairau Road, Auckland 10, New Zealand

Why are you reading this?

First published by Penguin Books Australia,
1987 Nihil obstat

Copyright © Santo Cilauro, Tom Gleisner, Rob Sitch, Andrew Knight,
John Alsop, Magda Szubanski, 1987

Typeset by Leader Composition Pty Ltd in Cheltenham, Memphis, English
Script, Times, Mead, Univers, Century, Hutchinson and Helvetica with the
handwriting of various artists and any old Letraset we had left over.
Made and printed by Australian Print Group, Maryborough using a very
large machine with levers on the side.

CIP

The D-generation bumper book of Aussie heroes.

ISBN 0 14 010482 8.

1. Australian wit and humor. 2. Profit making attempt following tv series –
excuse. I. Alsop, John. II. D-generation (Television series).

A828′.30208

TABLE OF CONTENTS

SPECIAL THANKS TO:

Trevor Johnston, Brendan Luno, Phil, John and Lee from EON-FM, Matthew Kelly and Santo's dog who went through so much for so little.

INTRODUCTION

Here at the Bicentennial Authority, it has been our aim
to commission projects of enduring worth. Already
many of you will be familiar with our Trent Nathan
toilet-seat covers or Brett Whiteley's haunting sets for
a poignant and provocative Bicentennial ballet, based
on the autobiography of Patrick White. But now, it is
our very great pleasure to launch, perhaps the pinnacle
of Australian artistic endeavour. At a cost of over one
million dollars per chapter, "The D-Generation
Bumper Book of Great Aussie Heroes".
Please, sit back, relax and enjoy.
You paid for it . . .

While the rest of Sydney sweltered today in 32°C heat, this lucky anti-drugs campaigner was spotted by our reporter taking a refreshing dip at Bondi Beach.

Dear Sir,
I love this country; and frankly, I hate people who criticise it. When I came here, I was poor – very poor – but through hard work and a lot of violence I made my way up in the drug trade. Now, thanks to the selective vigilance of the police, I'm able to live in luxury, send my kids to private schools, and I pay no taxes. In any other country I'd be thrown straight out of Parliament.

(Name & Address withheld by threat)
Yours

DISCOVERY OF AUSTRALIA

COOK We shall land soon, Joseph. There's always a certain excitement with discovery. Lands for the empire, eh, Banks?

BANKS You know, James, I've been thinking – perhaps we should just leave. Forget we ever found this place. We've already discovered New Zealand – two islands, lots of mountains, beautiful coastline. I'd say we're doing well.

COOK Are you saying we shouldn't claim this land, Joseph?

BANKS Well, what's going to happen, James? Colonisation, convicts? There are probably primitive but happy people here, living in harmony and amusing themselves with simple but effective musical instruments.

COOK No, no. I have a good feeling about this land.

BANKS There are no snakes in New Zealand.

COOK Look, I think this place is really going to take off. I can see it producing works of literature, music – great music, Joseph – that will delight the world.

I can see sheep, and stump-jump ploughs; and I can see things called supermarkets, and enormous furniture warehouses, and more. I can see lawn-mowers, panel-vans, mo'casins, wet T-shirt competitions, big bins. I can see my old cottage being shipped out here . . .

All right, maybe that sounds a bit crazy. But you know what I *can* see? Not now, but in two hundred years' time – a huge celebration of what this land stands for. Think of it, Banks; because of us, a bicentennial year!

BANKS Back to New Zealand?

COOK Alright.

> **SIR THOMAS BENT** *Victoria's popular premier from 1904 to 1909. Tommy's career was sadly marred by groundless allegations of corruption after he innocently re-routed the St Kilda tramline to pass land he just happened to have recently purchased.*

Dear Eds,

In recent weeks, a lot of baseless allegations have been levelled at me by you and your colleagues in the Gutter Press and I'd like to take them, if I may, in point form.

1) The 'alleged' tape. Now, surely the word 'heroin' appears in any normal dinner-party conversation. I notice the mud-slinging media conveniently neglected to quote such excerpts as 'pass the salt, Dennis' and 'More chablis?'. But one mention of the word 'heroin' (we were discussing Joan of Arc by the way) and immediately I'm running a racket!

2) The 'Mr Big' mentioned in this cock-and-bull tape. OK. You want to know about Mr Big? I'll tell you who Mr Big was. Mr Big just happened to be a clown at my youngest's birthday party. Senior Constable Murnane was his assistant, an extremely talented contortionist. And, speaking of my son, I don't mind the mud flying at me, but when you start attacking my loved ones! At no time, and this is point (3). At no time has my son ever taken drugs. He's always paid for everthing he uses. And I want that on record.

4) The alleged 'photograph' of the woman referred to as 'Miss Velvet Thighs'. Wrong! I repeat, wrong! *Doctor* Velvet Thighs, a leading Philipino skin specialist. (She was examining an eczema condition which I've always had in that particular area).

Finally 5) the alleged 'package. It just so happens that my wife – who is a very fine cook indeed – was preparing a chocolate cake, and required, naturally enough, 2½ kilos of baking soda. Now how was I to know that the man who approached me in the street would be selling anything else? I am appalled that this nation has reached the stage that it can no longer trust a member of its own police force.

Yours
F.X. O'Callaghan (Canberra)

ORIGAMI!!!

The ancient Japanese art of folding thin substances into any shape you like. Today, we fold a Queensland Government Minister into a swan.

Next week, we'll learn how to turn a rainforest into a multi-million dollar coastal resort!

THE JOY OF AUSSIE SEX

Let's face it – Australians have a marvellous reputation throughout the world as consummate lovemakers. Apparently we're described in Europe as 'molto monotoni'. And quite rightly too! Here, and over the next few pages, we take a look at some of the great moments in our sexual history...

'THE JOLLY ROGER'
POSITION 1:

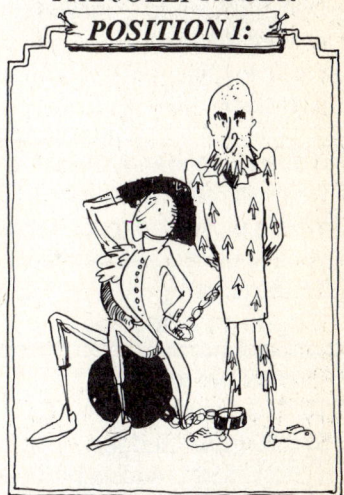

(Convict on bottom, British naval officer on top.)

1.

2.

3.

JEAN DE LA PEROUSE *A French naval officer, Jean was one of this country's first 'migrants', arriving to build a better life in Australia in January 1788. He left in March 1788.*

CENSUS

(To be completed by all Australians and Torres Strait Islanders – wherever the hell that is)

Name:
Address:
Where do you normally leave spare house key:
No. of occupants who spent last night in house:
(Does not include elderly relatives in a bungalow or tool shed)

Specify:
Children ☐
Spouse ☐
De facto ☐
Girl/boyfriend (your parents
will not be informed) ☐
One night stand (if stayed until
at least 2 a.m.) ☐
Was he/she a Torres Strait
Islander?

If one night stand, please specify:
Name (if remembered)
Where picked up (pub, Italian
youth club, nurses' home,
Torres Strait)
Did you go all the way? ☐

Income per week:
$0-$70 (loser) ☐
$76.80 (dole bludger) ☐
$76.81–$500 (Aussie battler) ☐
Over $500 (filthy rich bastard) ☐

Occupation:
Small businessman just trying
to keep his head above water
amidst the Keating/Hawke tax
madness. ☐
Other: ☐

Religion:
(Mick, Yid, Proddy, Democrat,
etc.)

If migrant, please specify:
Fish and chip shop owner ☐
Fruit and vegetable shop
owner ☐
Baroque furniture warehouse
owner ☐

Do you speak a language other than English?
No ☐
Jawolt/oui/si/jah/'k'n' oath ☐

How do you feel about having your privacy invaded every four years?
I think it is necessary ☐
It should be done every year ☐
Really fantastic, I love it and I
completely support the idea of
an Australia Card ☐

LEARN TO SPEAK FRENCH!

It's easy! Fun! Speak to people from France!

Many believe French is an extremely difficult language. But our course will have you conversing fluently in just *one hour*.
Here's an example to get you started.

Bon = good
Bon bons = mixed lollies
See? It's incredibly easy!!!
So send now for our easy-to-read instructional cassette.

Here's what a few people have said about the Speak-easy course:
'The Speak-easy course is bon.'
'It's the bonnest language course I ever did'.
'After just one lesson I can speak French really mixed lollies.'

4

```
18AP-               *        -02P39-    -   -
DEAR SHER SCH SCHER CHYR LUV,

        I AM WELL, HOW ARE YOU ? WELL, I HOPE.  HERE I AM IN OUTER
SPACE.  IT'S UNROOL.  I'M ROOL RAPPED TO BE HERE WITH PROWSEY.  WE'RE
HAVING A ROOL RAGE.  SPACE IS MUCH BETTER THAN ALL THE PLACES WE EVER
GONE TO, EVEN MERIMBOOLA.  PROWSEY IS A GRATE BLOKE.  HE'S GOT A FORD
GT 351 '72 MODEL AND HE PROMISSED ME A RIDE BACK ON EARTH, SO I CAN'T
HARDLY WAIT.  YOU SHOULD HAVE SEEN WHAT PROWSEY DON  SORRY SHYR LUV,
MY PEN FLOATED AWAY.   ANYWAY, YESTERDAY PROWSEY STREAKED.  FIRST
STREAKER IN SPACE.  UNROOL, AY?  OH YEH, THESE SPACE SHUTTLE THINGS
ROOLLY MOVE.  LET ME TELL YA, THEY MOVE.  THIS IS ONE BEAUOOTIFUL
MACHINE.

I'M ROOL PROUD OF BEING THE FIRST AUSTRALIAN IN SPACE.  SO IS
PROWSEY.  OH YEAH, HE DROPPED A BROWN-EYE AT THE WORLD YESTERDAY.  IT
WAS HILER HELLOR VERY FUNNY.

HOW ARE THE KIDS ?  I HOPE YOU ARE TAKING SHAINE TO THE FOOTY.  HAS
HE STARTED WALKING YET ?

PROWSEY JUST FARTED.  WHAT A BLOKE AY ?  UNROOL.  HE RECKONS HIS WIFE
BRUISES EASILY TOO.

I LUV YOU, LUV.  AND MISS YOU SOMETHING BAD.  HAVE YOU BEEN CLEANING
THE CAR ?

BEEING AWAY FROM THE KIDS AND YOU FOR SO LONG HAS ROOLY GOT ME
THINKING, AND IT MAKES ME RELIZE THAT NO MATTER HOW MUCH OF AN UNROOL
RAGE TIME I'M HAVING UP HERE, THERE'S ONLY ONE PLACE WHERE IT ALL
ROOLY COUNTS.  THE PUB.

            SEE YA SOON,

            WAI WAN WARN

                xxx

P.S.  PROWSEY FARTED AGAIN.
```

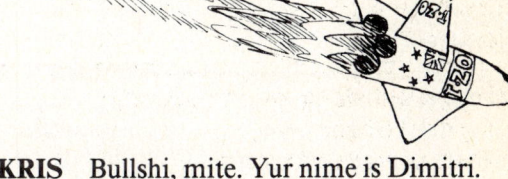
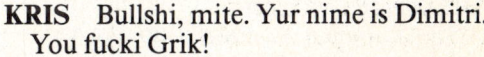

DIMITRI DOES HIS BACK
(A Greek Tragedy in one act)

KRIS   Hhhhhhey, Dimitri. Why you no fucki went to the fucki socca hon fucki Sunday?

DIMITRI   Hhhhh-I donno, re. My back hoort.

KRIS   Fucki bastard! Yoor boss muss be ha rill malacca poofta!

DIMITRI   No, re. Hiss my folt.

KRIS   Bullshi, mate. Fucki woork too hard. You go to Woorka Compesasho. You get money. Buy some fucki flats.

DIMITRI   Hhhhhey, Kris. You think this scripp is-a fucki rycist?

KRIS   For shur, malacca. Fucki poofta university kids write. Neva even see ha fucki socca gime hin thay fucki life.

DIMITRI   Hhhey, Kris. Whhhy hhh-I tork like-a this? Hhh-I'm-a not even Grik.

KRIS   Bullshi, mite. Yur nime is Dimitri. You fucki Grik!

DIMITRI   My nime is Russell, malacca. Hhhh-I was fucki born hin Hoodnadatta.

KRIS   Fucki hell! You hin tha wronn scripp!!

DIMITRI   Oi, re. You think is malacca university pooftas like me tork like-a this?

KRIS   Yes, mite.
Hhhey, re. Hh-I hev a fucki plan. This malacca pooftas-they give you some fucki drachmas to be hin this fucki scripp?

DIMITRI   For shu, Kris. Hh-I got pay five dolla.

KRIS   Fucky byoodi, mite! They you fucki boss, right?! They fuck you voice–hey gotta pay you Worka-fucki Compesasho!!!

DIMITRI   Bluddy Jizuz, mite! You a fucki jinius.

CAROLINE CHISHOLM *Pioneer social worker remembered for her tireless efforts on behalf of single Australian girls, and for establishing this country's first crèche.*

PROSPECTUS:

From the makers of Macarthur – King of the Merino comes . . .

CAROLINE CHISOLM – THE WOMAN

(A feature film)

SYNOPSIS:
Caroline, an English migrant, arrives in Australia and meets up with Bluey (Kirk Douglas) who leads her wagon train across the Arizona desert to Adelaide. There they meet a delightful Aboriginal chieftain (Eddie Murphy) who reveals a surprising secret against the panoramic backdrop of the great Australian bush.

A NOTE FROM THE WRITER:
'Epic' is a much-abused word amongst writers and visonaries, but I feel that *Caroline Chisolm – The Woman* truly justifies that title.

A NOTE FROM THE PRODUCER:
'Money spinner' is a much-abused phrase within investment circles, but I feel that with the 10BA provisions this film falls neatly into that category.

THE DIRECTOR
Phil Eastman is one of the most experienced film makers in the country. His past credits highlight the special interest he holds for people on Australian banknotes.

1979 *Joseph Banks – Man Behind the Green Thumb*
1980 *John Farrer – Groping for Grain* (Winner of Australian Farmers' Federation Prix D'honneur).
1982 *The Platypus – Monotreme To a Nation*

EASTMAN ON 'CHISOLM'
What first grabbed me about Chisolm was its sheer brilliance. I was amazed that no one had ever thought of doing a film based on an Australian historical event before. I mean, in 1850, two guys camel-trained it to the Gulf of Carpentaria – now there *has* to be a film in that. Ever think of the ice-cream spin-offs! Well, maybe it's a bit boring . . .

INT: The story is set on the docks in Sydney, yet you're shooting it in the Pacific Islands. Why?

PHIL: I know this may sound crazy, but the Pacific is more Sydney than Sydney. Maybe its the light or something.

INT: It added three million dollars to the cost.

PHIL: I told you it would sound crazy.

INT: Did you have trouble casting the film?

PHIL: None whatsoever. I read the book, I read the screenplay and there's Chisolm – this crazy, zany, quintessential woman. I had Chisolm on my mind and, all of a sudden, I'm seeing Sigrid Thornton. I'm thinking Chisolm, I'm seeing Thornton. I called in Graham, and he said 'Siggy, it just has to be'.

INT: Why then choose the American actress Madge Cruickshank?

PHIL: Siggy was unavailable. In a sense though, Madge is even more Chisolm than Siggy.

INT: You look at the cast, and think of names like Jack Thompson, Sam Neil, Bryan Brown.

PHIL: Yes you do, it's a pity they were unavailable too.

INT What does 'Chisolm' mean to you?

PHIL: I like to think of words like integrity, honesty, quality.

INT: You see them in the project?

PHIL: No . . . but I think about them . . . a lot.

JOHN MACARTHUR *One of our true heroes, this pioneer pastoralist went to England for eight years, leaving his wife Elizabeth to raise seven children, manage the farm and develop the finest merino flock in Australia. Upon his return in 1817, John accused her of infidelity, ended the marriage and took up his rightful place as founder of Australia's wool industry.*

COMING HOME

G'day Marge, where's Jamie? What do you mean, 'he's run away from home?' I just bought him a football. What am I gonna do with a spare football? I'm too fat to do any sport. You're a woman, you can't use it. Why don't you think before you act? That boy was the only thing I could kick apart from you and the dog. Now what am I gunna do? Take it out on the wogs? There are laws against that. I should never have married you. All my mates told me you were stupid, I just thought you were ugly. Give me a break luv, I know you're only a woman; I've accepted that but for Christ's sake, that doesn't mean you have to behave like an idiot all your life. Now shut up; get off your arse, get me some tea and behave like a human being for once. Bloody feminists . . .

DINNER IS SERVED

What's this then? I'm not eating no dago trash. All I want is raw steak and crushed spuds. And don't start with that cholesterol tripe. Next you'll be telling me I can't go to the pub, get drunk, beat you up and rape you every night. Now look, don't start fiddlin' with the natural order of things. You see it's like this: I'm a man I work hard, you're a woman, you're stupid. I come home hungry as a half-starved boong, and you tell me it's our anniversry. You suggest we eat wog food, I suggest a minute's silence. Now don't get me wrong, Marge; I respect you as an object, but if God had meant women to think he would have given them a brain. Now for Christ's sake, shut your trap, get up, stop bawlin' and cook me some real food. Bloody feminists . . .

A QUIET NIGHT

Christ, Marge, get out of my chair. A man comes in from the dunny to find his wife acting like an irresponsible tart and sitting in his good chair. Now shut up and don't explain, 'cos I'm not gunna listen. What do you think you are anyway? An individual? get serious, love; I only married you 'cos you had big norgs, and they shrivelled up after you had the kid. Now get off your barge arse and . . . (HEAD EXPLODES DUE TO 5 KILOS OF TNT)

A QUIET NIGHT Pt 2 (The Courtroom)

The man was a pig your Honour, he was unbearable. I tried to please him, but it made no difference. I just couldn't take it anymore.

Decision

You couldn't take it anymore? How do you think I feel, come in from the dunny and find some irresponsible tart sitting idiotically in my court; get serious love . . .
     Guilty!
     Bloody feminists . . .

Le Tampon – for that 'Ring of Confidence'

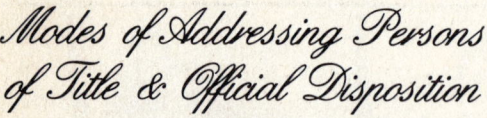

Modes of Addressing Persons of Title & Official Disposition

H.M. THE QUEEN

When speaking to the Queen, use 'Your Majesty' at first, then 'Elizabeth' or 'Lizzie'. When a guest at Buckingham Palace, the correct mode is 'Mrs Windsor'.

QUEEN MOTHER

Begin by attracting her attention, then speak loudly and clearly, 'He-llo Your Maj-esty. Would you like your rug?

ARCHDEACON

Begin with 'Venerable Sir', and avoid swallowing his ring. Wife – no title.

ROMAN CATHOLIC BISHOP

'My Lord' or 'Your Lordship'. Wife – pretend you didn't notice her. Try to avoid conversation topics like abortion and the Australian dollar.

GOVERNOR GENERAL

'Your Excellency' or 'Your Sobriety'.

Speeches

The Preamble: the list should be kept as short as possible, subject to avoiding any omission which may cause offence. Should the Queen be present always begin with, 'May it please Your Majesty . . .'; should an IRA member also be present, the preamble begins with, 'Run like hell'. It is then usual to commence with a joke. The one about the three nuns and a soap manufacturer is an old favorite with royalty.

The Ending: A speaker proposing a toast, should make this intention clear at the end such as, 'I give you the toast of . . .', 'I ask you to raise your glasses and drink to . . .', or 'skull, skull, skull.'

Formal Wear

GENTLEMEN

Morning dress consists of black top hat, yellow chamois gloves, patent leather or calf Oxford shoes and a plain doeskin waistcoat. In short, no less than three (3) animals must have died for a complete night out.

LADIES

Formal wear consists of long or short dresses, along with furs and leather shoes. Boob tubes are right out. Strict rules apply to the wearing of gloves. Very long or very short gloves are worn with short-sleeved or sleeveless outfits; with three-quarter length sleeves, gloves should reach the sleeve, and should overlap slightly. Long white kid gloves are usually worn in the presence of royalty, and it is correct practice to leave them on when dancing or in a receiving line; but to remove them entirely when eating, and to remove one when visiting the lavatory.

Right royal embarrassment as THE QUEEN is caught naked in the back seat of a popular night club performer's car!!!

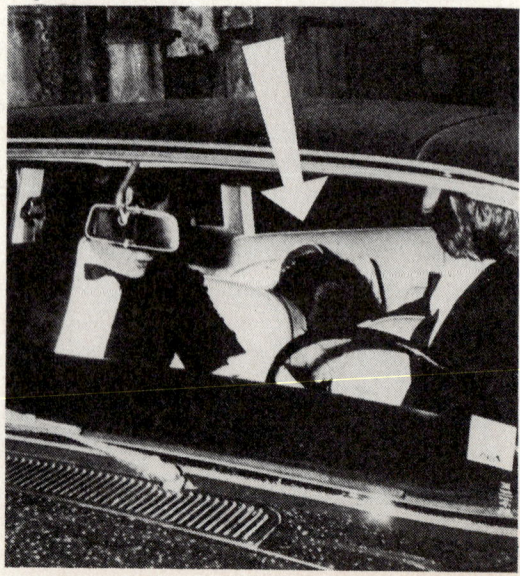

HENRY JAMES O'FARRELL *An extreme Irish nationalist who lived in Sydney, O'Farrell earns a place in the history of this great country as the first Australian to attempt the assassination of a visiting British monach. He failed; the Duke of Edinburgh lived, and Ireland remains without home rule.*

BLACKBURN PHILATELIC SOCIETY
Minutes of Monthly Meeting

Present
Brian Murnane (President)
Kathy Bartwell (Secretary)
Geoff Oslen
Paul Rutlidge
Josef Stalin Bader-Meinhoff (New Member)
Fyodor Chè Guevara Stanislovsky (New Member)

APOLOGIES
Marcus Brentsome (cut his finger on a Mexican Swordfish stamp. Finger and stamp are all right).

MOTIONS
Brian (Pres) proposed that a card be sent to Marcus from the Society, wishing him a speedy recovery. (Passed: 3-2)

Brian (Pres) further proposed that his North Solomon Island Gila Fish stamp go on display in the club rooms. (Passed: 3-2)

Joseph (new member) proposed that the Blackburn Philatelic Society declare its support for Col. Gadaffi's Middle East policy. (Defeated: 2-3)

Fyodor (new member) proposed that the BPS immediately poison Canberra's water supply as a gesture of solidarity with the Nicaraguan rebels. (Defeated: 2-3)

Josef (new member) proposed that the chairman of the Blackburn Philatelic Society be immediately shot, and that the club's assets be divided amongst the remaining members. (Passed: 5-0)

Brian shot 9.35 pm
Meeting closed 9.40 pm

Kathy Bartwell (President)

Exclusive, new evidence of Prince Charles' Nazi connections.

JOHN BATMAN *The plucky colonist who purchased 600,000 acres of Melbourne land from Aborigines in return for mirrors, blankets and beads. The contract of sale he drew up was agreed to by the brothers Jaga Jaga, Jaga Jaga and Jaga Jaga (formerly of Collins St.).*

CONVEYANCING: TWENTY REASONS WHY YOU NEED A SOLICITOR.

ONE: DRESS SENSE
How many do-it-yourself conveyancing kits come in a three-piece suit or twin set?

TWO: PEACE OF MIND
Only when you've forked out $2,000 for what is essentially a routine commercial transaction can you really be sure of getting it right.

THREE: TRAINING
Every solicitor has spent at least four years at university, getting pissed at the taxpayers expense. So you can be sure that, when his/her secretary handles the entire affair, your solicitor will remember to at least cast an eye over it sometime after lunch.

FOUR: EQUITIES OF ACQUIESCENCE
These are claims over land dating back to feudal times when Charles V decreed certain estates to be easements in perpetuity. Now, can you really trust a do-it-yourself kit to detect whether a Tudor Monarch has a claim in equity over your brick veneer in Balmain?

FIVE TO NINETEEN
Take our word for it, we're lawyers.

TWENTY FINALLY
All solicitors subscribe to a general insurance scheme. That means if one of our word processing girls does stuff it up, you then have to get involved in further costly litigation to assert your somewhat ill-defined rights. Ever heard of one lawyer testifying against another?

SIR REDMOND BARRY *Judge, statesman and founder of Melbourne University, Sir Redmond was a moral guiding light of early Australia, delivering his often harsh sentences with an unswerving sense of justice. The name of his mistress was Mrs Louisa Barrow.*

KOORYAL LEARNING CO-OPERATIVE
<u>Minutes of Teachers' Meeting (Wed. 4 June)</u>

PRESENT: Barry, Jenny, Graeme, Simon and Trish
APOLOGIES: Siobhan (had a previous Tai-chi commitment)

The meeting began with our school plumber, Warren, rushing into the staff room, requesting permission to make an announcement.

> <u>For</u>: Barry, Graeme, Simon, Trish.
> <u>Qualified</u>: Jenny (who felt, as a woman, that she would listen to Warren's announcement, but that she would not necessarily agree with it).

This qualification was unanimously supported.

After formal permission was granted and Jenny's qualification noted, Warren proceeded to announce that the school's plumbing had exploded. No one quite saw any significance in this fact. Warren seemed to get quite excited, so Graeme asked how everyone fitted into this 'sewerage scenario' of his. Warren replied, 'Up to the knees.'

At this point, Jenny moved an objection, feeling (as a woman) that Warren was being confrontationalist. She further wanted it recorded that she had been teaching for ten years and did not have to put up with this sort of thing. We all agreed that Warren was displaying hostility, and Trish suggested that maybe he was talking crap. Warren agreed.

When the main boiler exploded, Warren said that we were about to meet the problem head on. Barry suggested we bring the kids in on this one and perhaps make a video. This idea was unanimously supported, and it was decided that the whole issue was simply a question of semantics – a lot of words. Warren at least agreed it rhymed with that.

After Warren left, the meeting continued with the main discussion of the afternoon – which pupil not to punish this week.

JACKEY JACKEY *One of Australia's best-loved black citizens, Jackey Jackey was awarded a government gratuity for his services to this country and sent back to his tribe near Albany. There he died peacefully during a wild drinking spree, when he fell on to a fire and burned to death.*

The Australian bicentennial celebrations are still many months away. Yet already these 'First Australians' are busy preparing for the exciting street parties . . .

. . . the many performing arts spectaculars . . .

. . . and a myriad of other community events . . .

. . . all making up the dazzling programme which will honour two hundred years of civilisation on these rugged shores.

For black Australians, the bicentennial means a chance to become part of the broader family of Australians; to hold their heads up high. . .

. . . and say 'Thank you'.

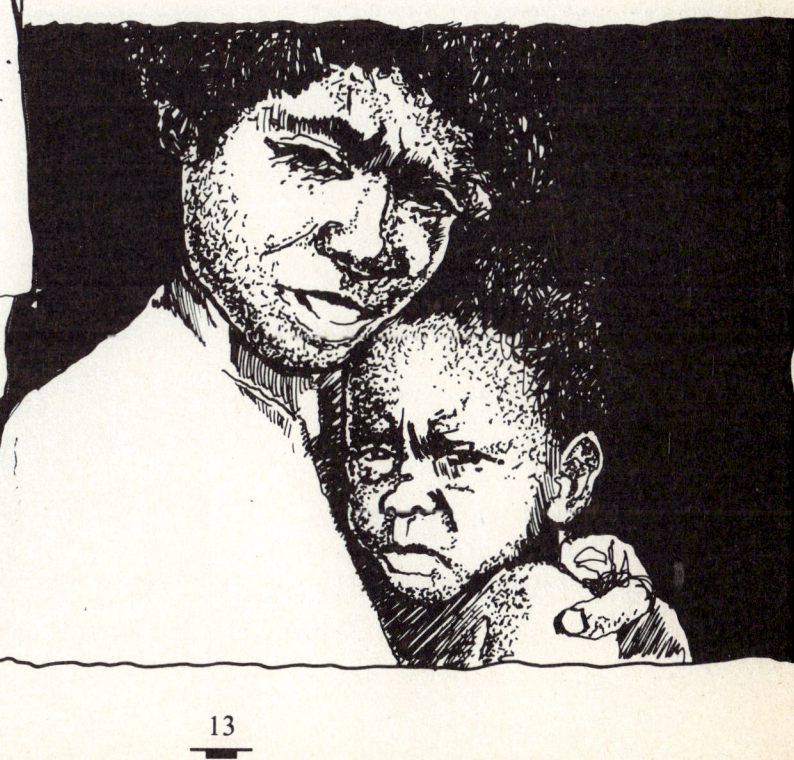

STUDENT ACTION!!!
(OFFICIAL MAGAZINE OF THE BURKE UNIVERSITY STUDENTS UNION)

Labour Club.

In a shock move last week, Peter Watson of the student ALP Club declared that he had split with the Centre Left Unity Faction (CLU) and was now an official delegate of the Labor Club's Moderate Right Alliance (MRA). However, a spokesperson for the CLU has declared that as far as s/he is/are concerned Peter Watson was never a member of the CLU but rather a non-union-affiliated nominee for the Broad Unity Collective (BUC). The issue is bound to cause fireworks at next Thursday's general meeting, and is of vital concern to all politically aware students. The SRC are organising badges.

LIBERAL CLUB.

Cocktail party tonight. Ring Lachlan for details.

FEMINIST CLUB.

Wine and cheese tasting tonight in the Womyn's room. Those interested please contact Olga in her usual cubicle, to arrange seating.

BENNY HILL APPRECIATION SOCIETY.

Special stunt of the week. We covered the letters 'WO' in the 'WOMEN'S TOILETS' sign so that men would walk right in. Strangely, no girl in French lingerie came running out. Just a woman in overalls who threw a cheese platter at us.

ANARCHIST CLUB.

Smash capitalism rally postponed because Comrade Stovlasky (Geoff Miller) has an Advanced Administrative Law lecture.

CHRISTIAN FELLOWSHIP.

Lonely, insecure people completely lacking in social skills wanted to join our club. Come and hear Roy McArdle give his amazing testimony about how Jesus Christ has changed his life. Theatre A, 1 p.m.

Rory O'Dwyer – lucky winner of *The University's* "receive a piece of stale bread from a cardboard cutout" competition.

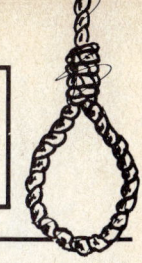

> **JAMES BARRET** *The first person to be executed in the lucky country, Jim went to the gallows for robbery at the age of seventeen.*

INSIDE STUDENT ACTION

- **Another bloody article about sexual harrassment**
- Peter Watson hits back at the Centre left
- 20 hard-hitting Reagan jokes
- **Caf dispute threatens world peace**
- English library declared nuclear free
- **Sexist course titles: 'Chemical engineering 1B' to be changed to 'Chemical Engineering and Women 1B'**
- The Centre left and Peter Watson: where to now?
- **Editor's plea: can I get a cadetship with a major Australian daily?**

ENGINEERING STUDENTS.

Pub night. Get pissed and beat up Asian students for being smarter than us.

ATHEISTS SOCIETY.

Theatre A, 1.05 p.m. (back entrance). Meet in devil costumes.

DON'T FORGET!!! UNION NITE NEXT SUNDAY.

Bands:
Laughing Ashtrays.
Hey Bill, I'm Milk. (Koorie youth band)
Gin Wahn Flange.
And three other totally forgettable bands vying for the most pretentious name.
PLUS GUEST ACT!!!
Top folk/pop protest fivesome – Redgum. Singing hard-hitting, controversial songs from their latest album 'Ban Conscription Fraser'.
$5 Burke Students
$6 cripples, retards, paros etc
$8 anyone else stupid enough to come

THE JOY OF AUSSIE SEX
'The Straight A'

POSITION 23:

(Arts student with overdue essay on bottom, Vice Chancellor on top.)

JOHN AINSWORTH HORROCKS *South Australia's tragic explorer. John accidentally shot himself whilst unloading a gun from a kneeling camel. Only twenty-eight years old, Horrocks was brave, good-looking and could well have been one of this country's greatest pioneers. As it is, he is remembered as the only South Australian to be shot by a reclining dromedary.*

Events that forged a Nation

As every schoolboy knows, world history is the story of great men and their deeds and the history of Australia reads like the greatest adventure story ever told, because the heroes are real men and their brave deeds are FACTS.

1788   End of the paleozoic era

1789   The bodies of dead aborigines found lying in coves around Port Jackson indicate the introduction of smallpox into Australia, the first in a long series of exciting new European diseases.

1878   A cyclone hits Darwin, damaging every building in town.

1897   A cyclone hits Darwin, more severe than any before.

1914   Australia comes of age by facing 'the one trial that all humanity still recognises, . . . the test of a great war' (C.E.W. Bean, Official War Historian).

1915   7,000 boys between the ages of seventeeen and twenty-one fail to come of age on a beach in Turkey. As every schoolboy knows, Gallipoli was one of the most important defeats in Australian history; it meant that we could once and for all, and with great dignity, hold our head up among fellow nations as an extremely important colony.

(Nothing of great significance happened in the following years until . . .)

1970 | A 'great mark' in history was made by Alex Jesaulenko in the VFL Grand Final. (Some experts would say that the mark taken by Ian Scott in the 1968 Final was the most spectacular but this honour is traditionally accorded to Jesaulenko because it was the first such mark by a 'New Australian', heralding a new era of 'multi-culturalism' in the rich tapestry of Australian Rules Football.)

1971 | The nation is divided by a split in Mrs Sonia McMahon's dress. While some considered such attire inappropriate for the wife of a Prime Minister, others saw this display of 'extremely attractive' legs as the hallmark of our new sophistication.

1972 | Flamboyant South Australian Premier Don Dunstan wears a pair of candy pink shorts into Parliament. Though Australians are an extremely 'broad-minded' people, many thought that this 'sort of thing' should not be tolerated. However, the Premier was graciously allowed to remain in office. This is because Australia is a pluralist society which can accommodate shorts of all colours, shapes and sizes.

1974 | Top secretary Juni Morosi is drawn into public life when the Liberal Opposition discreetly hint that she rose through unusual means – and that they (the Liberals) had been left out. Such open and free exchange of information is the basis of a healthy democracy. Also in the same year, a cyclone hits Darwin, followed by Bill and Boyd and a two-part Mini-Series.

1975 | A bridge spanning Tasmania's Derwent River runs into the bulk carrier *Lake Illawarra*, killing twelve people. The dismissal of Australia's socialist Labor Government in the same year gives many people 'pause for thought', allowing them to reconsider the hasty, ill-informed election choice they had made in 1972.

1977 | The Granville Railway disaster leaves eight-three dead, 213 injured and over 500 very late for work.

1988 | A bicentenary hits Darwin (no survivors).

17

REVEREND ROBERT STEEL One of Australia's best-read authors, his works include Doing Good; or the Christian in Walks of Usefulness *(1858)*, Lives Made Sublime by Faith and Work *(1861)*, Burning and Shining Lights, or Memoirs of Good Ministers of Jesus Christ *(1864)*, and Shagging on The Sabbath *(unpublished)*.

Around The Pews, with Fr Barry

Papal Poaching

With the number of vocations steadily falling in the Catholic Church, it's a pity to see that various religious orders have resorted to openly poaching clerics from one another. The biggest offenders are the Redemptionist Monks and Marist Brothers, who last year both exceeded their salary caps by recruiting over twenty novitiates from WA. Meanwhile, the Jesuits and Dominicans have been battling over the fate of one Brother Patrick O'Keene, a Melbourne scholastic. O'Keene, who trained last year with the Sydney Salesians, is now seeking a Papal clearance so he can pray with a Jesuit team here in Melbourne. This row shouldn't affect his selection in tomorrow's State of Original Sin Mass to be held at St Patrick's. Asked about the overall lack of young recruits, sources high up in the Catholic League have blamed poor training facilities, a drop in the level of Sunday spectators, and the fact that priests still aren't permitted to reproduce.

Text for the Last Shopping Day of Christmas

And the Lord told this parable: 'Have you heard the one about the beggar on his way to Damascus? There were these three guys, right, an Irishman, an Englishman, and a Jew . . .

Sister Therese's Video Guide

This week's choice: *Last Tango In Paris*

Though I enjoy a good travel movie as much as the next novitiate, this was a real disappointment. Slow dialogue, poor acting and one scene involving a disgraceful waste of dairy products. I gave it a 🕯🕯🕯🕯 (3½ candles)

Overheard in Confessional:

'Father, I've been having impure thoughts again.' 'Be strong, Sister Marie.'

DIAL-IT INFORMATION SERVICES

Dial-a-Religious Fanatic; hear them rave on and on about how Jesus Christ has changed their insignificant lives — 0666

Dial-an-Obscenity — XXXX

Dial-a-Public Servant (Not a record service but it might as well be) — Look under Govt.

Dial-a-Dick Joke — 6969

Drug Advisory Line; where to buy, current street prices — 000 11444

Dial-a-Top 40 Hit; as reproduced in full stereophonic sound by phone receiver — 1986.

Dial a Disco Hit — 1970.

Dial-a-Brandenburg Concerto — 1638.

Dial-an-Aussie Cricket Champ South Africa — 27 11 72045.

I MET GOD

A new book by Kevin Stanwyck, Bed 17, Longview Psychiatric Hospital.

I WAS WITH HIM

A supplement by Cyril Sinclair, Bed 18, Longview Psychiatric Hospital.

I AM GOD

God, Bed 19, Longview Psychiatric Hospital.

CRUCIFIX TOURS!!

Visit the Holy Land! Walk in Christ's Footsteps! Bethlehem, Jerusalem, Mount Sinai, Bali; all for the one incredibly low price (including airfare and twin share stable) You'll travel in air-conditioned coach comfort, complete with personal Holy Water fonts and forty other Religious fanatics just like yourself!

The Tour will be led by Monsignor Barry Barnes, one of our most experienced and sober coach drivers.

FEATURES: (not offered on many more expensive Protestant tours)
- VIEW THE BETHLEHEM DIORAMA!
- PAN FOR SAINTS BONES
- GRASS SKI DOWN MT CALVARY!
- TOUCH REAL LEPERS!

Book now and you will receive FREE a Crucifix Tours Travel-bag, complete with Bible, map of the Holy Land, and handy Shroud of Turin moistened towelettes.

GO REBUILD MY FAITH

Men who are interested in a life of service and who seek to live the gospel life in poverty, chastity and obedience are needed today. Contact your nearest Army Career's Advisor.

MOTHER ANGELICA'S LATIN LUST LINE

Phone me now for:
- Rosaries
- Gospel Readings
- Lives of the Saints
- Bedtime Prayers

Discretion assured.
All major holy cards accepted.
Si parla Italiano!

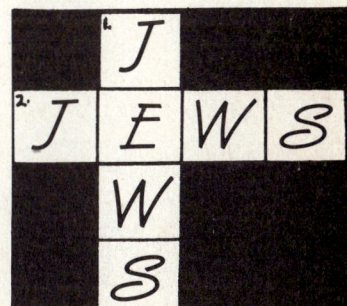

Chalice For Sale

Slightly damaged, will sell for $30 o.n.o. Ideal for parties – be the perfect host! (Get it?)

Text for Tomorrow

And Peter spoke unto the Mother of God: 'Grieve not Mary. Three days have now passed, let me roll away the rock. It's a new car!!!

Mark 3.14

TEXT FOR TUESDAY WEEK

And the Lord said, 'Never let women be priests – they're too stupid'

Revelations 7.23

ACKNOWLEDGEMENTS

Grateful thanks to St Jude for many prayers answered.

Grateful thanks to St Jude for all your help.

Pissed Off. Call yourself a saint? 'Rosie's Choice' didn't even *look* like winning.

BIGOT'S CROSSWORD

Across
1. Who killed the Son of God? (4)

Down
2. They killed Jesus. The .... (4)

	J		
J	E	W	S
	W		
	S		

ROBERT O'HARA BURKE

When the totally inexperienced Irish policeman was chosen to lead an expedition across Australia from south to north, many thought he would fail. But the Victorian Government, who organised the lavish and costly venture, had faith in the pioneering spirit of one Robert O'Hara Burke. He died under a tree near Coopers Crossing.

POST CARD

SURFERS' PARADISE
The shops, Le magasins,
Los negotiados, Gli empori.

Dear Henry,

12/9/86

We're all having an absolute BALL! Wrote to tell you I've just read the terrible news about your family in the paper. Its pretty bad luck. Have they caught the killer yet? I hope they can get fingerprints from the sledgehammer. I hope Maggie gets out of her coma! Shirley sends her regards - she reckons Maggie's sun-hat has come in real handy. She's a great woman, your wife — lets hope she doesn't become a quadraplegic. Jeez - you look really good in the pictures mate! Shirl and I were arguing about whether it was Sarah in the corner or Jason. Even though a blanket was thrown over them I reckon it was Sarah because of the teddy-bear next to her. You can tell me when I get back tomorrow week (try & hold off the funerals if you can- we'd LOVE to be there). Henry, now that most of your family's dead, do you reckon we could have your caravan - it'd come in handy! Also your finals tickets. My kid's love to go. I still can't believe the gall of that killer. Of all the people in Melbourne, why did he have to pick on your family to murder. Still, you can't blame these people really. They probably come from broken homes. Lets hope that they try and rehabilitate him when he's caught. Shirl says that if maggie dies, you're quite welcome to come on holidays with us next year. We're thinking of going to Merimbula. Should see all the sheilas there! You'd have a ball. Anyway I've got to pick the wife up at the shops. See you soon. By the way, I hope the bastard didn't take anything from the garage while he was there. I know a bloke who got his drill stolen! Some people are inconsiderate bastards! Your brother-in-law, Jack. P.S. You still owe me ten bucks.

HENRY CLARK ~~& FAMILY~~
27 WOODBANK DVE,
NUNAWADING.
3509.
(VICTORIA).

A bevy of beauties!!!

Are you sick of being left out of the 'in crowd'? Then have we got a place for you . . .

Dag City, unlicensed family discotheque.

Dance with the opposite sex!!!

Listen to the latest pop tunes, spun by our casually-dressed disc jockeys.

Meet other well-groomed youngsters with interesting hobbies.

Geoff congratulates Keith on his smart slacks.

'Do you collect model aeroplanes too?'

So, come to Dag City! All you need is an adventurous spirit, a spiffy pair of shiny brown shoes and a note from either Mum or Dad, and you can bossa nova till the wee small hours of the afternoon. Then have a nice, long nap . . .

My New Book

RONA Jilly . . . thanks very much for joining us tonight. You must be absolutely thrilled with your new book.

JILLY Absolutely, Nancy. I couldn't be happier. I have a lovely husband, a beautiful daughter – and I've just finished my first book!

RONA This marks a change of direction for you, doesn't it?

JILLY Yeah. I've always thought of myself primarily as an actress, but this was something I very much wanted, *needed* to do. A book was . . . I just knew I had to do it. And it wasn't easy.

RONA Why is that?

JILLY I had to re-organise my life completely, and commit myself totally to the book.

RONA I admire you for that. It must have taken a lot of courage.

JILLY Yes, it did.

RONA How long did this rigorous schedule go on for?

JILLY Well, I worked on it for at least ten hours a day for ten months.

RONA That's a lot of time.

JILLY Yeah. And it's changed me. I've discovered strengths – inner resources in me that I never knew I had.

RONA Can you tell us what it's about?

JILLY Hollywood basically; the glamour and the corruption behind the glamour.

RONA That's a familiar theme. What's it called?

JILLY *Hollywood Wives.*

RONA *Hollywood Wives!* You didn't write that! Jackie Collins did.

JILLY Write it? Oh no, I didn't *write* it. I *read* it. It's the first book I've ever read.

PETER KOCAN *Australia's first would-be political assassin, Kocan fired a shotgun at opposition leader Arthur Calwell in 1966. Calwell was unharmed, his chin absorbing much of the blast and Kocan was sentenced to life imprisonment. He was released after ten years and is now well regarded in Australian literary circles.*

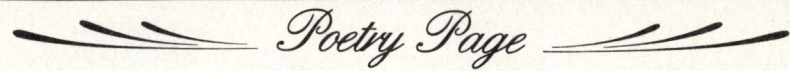

Poetry Page

DAWN

Still,
The morning sun draws rays
Into the blindness of my mind.
and still,
I write – this poem of life.
A line begins and ends
Then begins again
A comma,
Mispelt wurds – bad, punctuation
A
complete
waste
of
lines
Why oh why spells . . . yoy.

THIS POEM WINS $10!!!

THE EAGLE

He clasps the crag with crooked hands;
Close to the sun in lonely lands,
Ring'd with the azure world, he stands.

The wrinkled sea beneath him crawls;
He watches from his mountain walls,
And like a thunderbolt he farts.

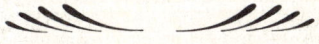

LIMERICK

A king named Oedipus Rex
Liked having sex
A lot.

THIS POEM WINS $20!!!

THEATRE REVIEW

It was bold, it was stark, it was the culmination of Adelaide's week long artistic festival. It was the Norwood Primary School's 5th Annual Nativity Play. And what an epic production! A cast chosen from over fifty Grade Two's and Three's, intensive workshopping and rigid toilet training all led to a performance which was nothing short of spectacular. Adrian Tsaris as Joseph came across as a brooding, intense patriarch, despite difficulties keeping his beard on. His often untucked shirt served as a poignant reminder of the ever-widening gulf between church and state which the play so ably conveyed. As for Felicity McNiece as Mary, what can I say that isn't summed up in the cry of one audience member – 'Don't pick your nose, Fiona'. This Grade Two milk monitor had the entire opening afternoon house of mums and dads actually *believing* she was a virgin. The second act began with a traditional flourish as the thirty-seven wise men somersaulted, vaulted and bounced over a cardboard manger (built by the Social Studies teacher, Mr Brandon) and into the wings. 'Have you any room in the Inn,' asked Joseph. 'No', replied the keeper (Mathew Duntrill); but there is room in this reviewer's heart for another superb production from the Norwood Junior Classes. *Bravo!*

"The Theatre, 2 hours before curtain"

"The Theatre, 20 minutes into performance"

PERCY ALDRIDGE GRAINGER One of Australia's greatest composers and self-flagellators, Grainger wrote many works, including the haunting 'The Warriors', a story of an Aboriginal corroboree for three grand pianos, full symphony orchestra, gongs, bells, marimbas and mallets used on piano strings. It is not frequently performed.

LADIES!!!

Is your womb letting you down?
Have you been childless for years
Because your ovum couldn't make an omelette???
THEN HAVE WE GOT A DEAL FOR YOU!!!

Introducing the revolutionary TEST TUBE-O-MATIC.®

Yes, this exciting new concept in home-bottling allows you to enjoy childbirth in the privacy of your own home, all year round.
Just look at what you get:

1 A uniquely contoured plastic womb, designed to fit anywhere. PLUS . . .

2 Half a litre of top grade sperm, hand-selected by our experts here at Brian's Seed Shop. PLUS . . .

3 Two dozen free range ovum.

NOW – How much would you expect to pay for this exciting home birth package??? Well, don't answer, because with TEST TUBE-O-MATIC® you also get a matching collander and obstetric knife set ABSOLUTELY FREE!!! So why wait – GESTATE!

Come and see us at Brian's Seed Shop and let ME impregnate YOU!!!

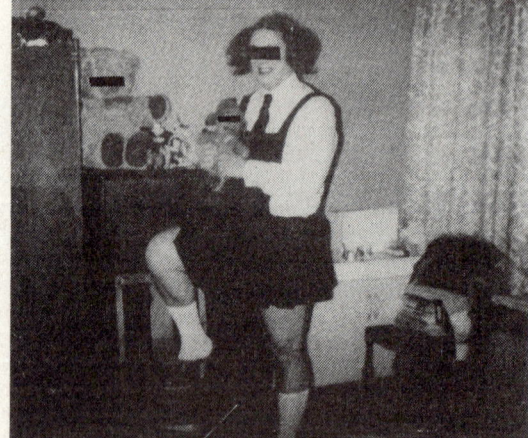

PICK - UP LINES

PICK-UP LINES

Recently a friend of mine said to me, 'Don, how come you always get lots of girls?' I said that apart from a good opening line, I don't do anything special. His next comment amazed me. 'I didn't know they worked.' Didn't know they worked!

I was stunned. No wonder he had lucked out. 'But, Don, people don't really use them, do they?' 'Of course they do,' I told him. That is exactly what girls want, they crave it.

I was further shocked to find that most of the other journos on the financial pages thought the same. Even our editor on *The Times* had *never* used one in his life. After talking to him for a couple of hours he asked me if I would write an article on the subject. 'Sure,' I said, 'it certainly seems to be a dying art.'

Before reading the following sample of lines it's essential to underline one thing. Girls love men who are assertive. By using an opening line you're saying that up front as well as showing your wit and charm. So when using these lines, believe in them and she'll believe in you. Read on and good luck!

'Is my tie straight? I'm going to an important meeting and I want to look just right.' (Use this in an elevator of a big office building. Girls love straightening ties.)

'Where'd you get that great hat?' (To any girl wearing a really zany hat.)

'You're Miss Ohio, aren't you? I saw a picture of you in the paper.' (This one is a surefire winner in Bendigo.)

'Here, let me carry that for you. I wouldn't want you to strain that lovely body of yours.' (Good line to a girl carrying an engine block.)

'You look sad'. (For girls at funerals.)

'What did you think of the play?' (For girls at the footy.)

'Would you like a push?' (Say this to girls in a wheelchair.)

'Instead of just sitting there looking bored, how about helping me gather some sea-shells?' (Perfect on public transport. Some friends swear by this one.)

'Are you following me?' (Say this to the girl you've been chasing all night.)

'Did you understand what the movie was about? I just couldn't follow it.' (Some people call this the death blow. If it's one thing women love to do, it's to explain *Rocky* movies.)

CLASSIFIEDS

Hi! I'm Candy. I'm randy. Phone me now – I'm a feminist.

CLUB NIRVANA For that special night out. A truly tasteful brothel for car salesmen who expect that extra touch of class. Discretion assured. Nothing anal.

HOT MAGAZINES All tastes catered for; wet nurse; Greek; shaved; leather; Tasmanian. Write now PO Box 117.

LONELY? Join our movie appreciation society. Meetings; back row of the Forum Cinema every Tues night. BYO groundsheet.

LOOKING FOR A PARTNER? We have Filipino ladies, many in the country right now. Clean, obedient and exotic. Best of all, these girls are too small to hit back.

FORD CORTINA '76. Low mileage, seeks casual or perm. relationship. Genuine offers only.

PUNY, ethnic looking but sincere premature ejaculator seeks foxy lady for up to 30 secs of good times.

WIFE SWAPPING Am prepared to trade a 32 year-old blonde, good condition, for a micro-wave.

PREGNANT? Need support? Our mobile scaffolding service can really take the strain off. Phone now for a no obligation measure and quote.

SINGLE? Pregnant? Need Support? The Catholic Counselling Centre offers supporting, caring advice to all potential murderesses.

VERY caring, deeply sensitive guy seeks tender woman for loving caring relationship. No Fatso's need apply.

GAY Comedian seeks straight man for comedy duo. PO Box 485.

A Consummate Recital Delights
Music with Quentin Connolly

In recent times it has become a simple task to predict the format of any recital by a visiting American ensemble. We are typically treated to a Beethoven sonata, a Bach partita and a Brahms concerto. But it was their failure to produce such an unadventurous repertoire that made The Iron Christ's concert here last week so refreshingly enjoyable.

The Heavy Metal band opened with 'Bleeding Brain', a work for three guitars and sledgehammer which suited their lyrical style – demonstrative and remote in turn. The lead guitars set up a whip-cracking pace during the early scherzo, highlighting the keyboard's sparkling surface and post-modernist undertones. And the drums were in time.

The next piece chosen in this most elegant of recitals was 'Murdering Slave' with its haunting allegro 'chucking vomit/chucking vomit chucking vomit, yeah . . .'. It had a far subtler tonal warmth than the opening piece and gave a filamentous tangibility to the whole recital. Yet, there was a lack of that resolute and elegant timbre we have become accustomed to from Roger 'Nasty' Crap's drumming and the final movement ('Voodoo Murder') was accomplished too hastily, with no breathing space for its clangorous, compelling grandeur. But the bravado and sheen of The Iron Christ's playing returned in 'Pus Salad' which closed the performance, eliciting cries of "bravo" from the appreciative audience, which abated only when the band returned for an encore and told them to 'piss off'.

The response to our Redgum/Goanna/Midnight Oil write a hard-hitting protest song competition has been fantastic. Here are just a few of the entries:

Myxamatosis is killing our bunnies
And US corporations think it's funnies.

        Susan R.

(Great, Susan. But it's a good idea to work out your rhyme first.)

No more dams for the Daintree
Let Franklin River whales swim free
No more bombs for Maralinga
Carn the Sydney Swans.

        Geoff H.

(Nice start, Geoff. It fades away a little at the end, though.)

Come all Australians where ever you stand
With a joint in your elbow and a bar in your hand
There's something going on, we're all implied
Last night another Queensland racehorse died.

        Adrien P.
(Fantastic!!! Really hard hitting.)

BumDrum

News, views and gossip from
the Australian rock scene.
Featuring . . . Bumdrum's Album of the Week

Rex, The Whistling Blue Heeler 'canine teardrops'

▪ Let Rex take you on

a trip down memory lane

with such numbers as

- ▪ 'You Ain't Nothing But a Hound Dog'
- ▪ 'I Woke Up In Luv This Morning'
- ▪ 'Rose of Spanial Harlem'
- ▪ 'Sexual Blue Heeling'
- ▪ 'My Rabies Comin' Home'
- ▪ 'Don't shit in the Subway'
- ▪ 'Canines for Africa'
- ▪ 'Smoke gets in your Guide Dog's Eyes'
- ▪ 'Please Releash Me'
- ▪ 'Shorthaired Pointer Sisters Medley'
- ▪ And for the children 'Puff the Magic Daschund'

PLUS!!! Special Bonus Offer buy
Volume 1 and get absolutely free. Vol 2
— Rex Whistle's Songs of Devotion!
'The Lord is My German Sheperd'
'Away in the Mange'
All this and more from Country and
Western's biggest canine star, Rex —
The Whistling Blue Heeler.

PLUS As a special offer to D-
Generation readers, we present this
FREE cut-out single, featuring Rex at
his best! Just carefully cut out the
lifelike replica of Rex, punch a hole in
the centre and put it on your turntable.
Then sit back and relax as you listen to
the sound of an expensive
stereophonic needle being dragged
across the page of a cheap Penguin
book printed on paper made from
Australian trees!!

29

PRIVATE ROBERT WEIR The Aussie soldier has a glorious reputation in battle and Private Robert Weir of the 4th Infantry Co was no exception. He has the honour of being our nation's first serviceman to die in active service in an Australian uniform. He wasn't shot – he just got sick.

For all we know, the
next war may be years and years
away . . .

Yet, already, these eager
veterans can almost savour
the first whiff of new
battles in far-off lands.

How well they recall their
last homecoming . . .
when tickertape and glory
showered down upon them . . .

like defoliant mixed
with warm jungle rain.

Their hearts still sing
with gratitude for the
subsequent years of full
employment . . .

the homes fit for heroes . . .

and the gleaming hospital
complexes where they can
take their newborn children
for specialised medical
services.

Next time, Australia calls, her veterans
will know what to do.

THE AGE

ROYAL COMMISSION CLEARS AGENT ORANGE

Will you?

SIR CHARLES KINGSFORD-SMITH One of the great pioneers of civil aviation, 'Smithy' is remembered as the first Australian to fly non-stop from London without being affected by a baggage handlers' dispute. Only the slow development of the packaging industry prevented him from also setting the first tinnie-drinking record for the UK-Australia flight.

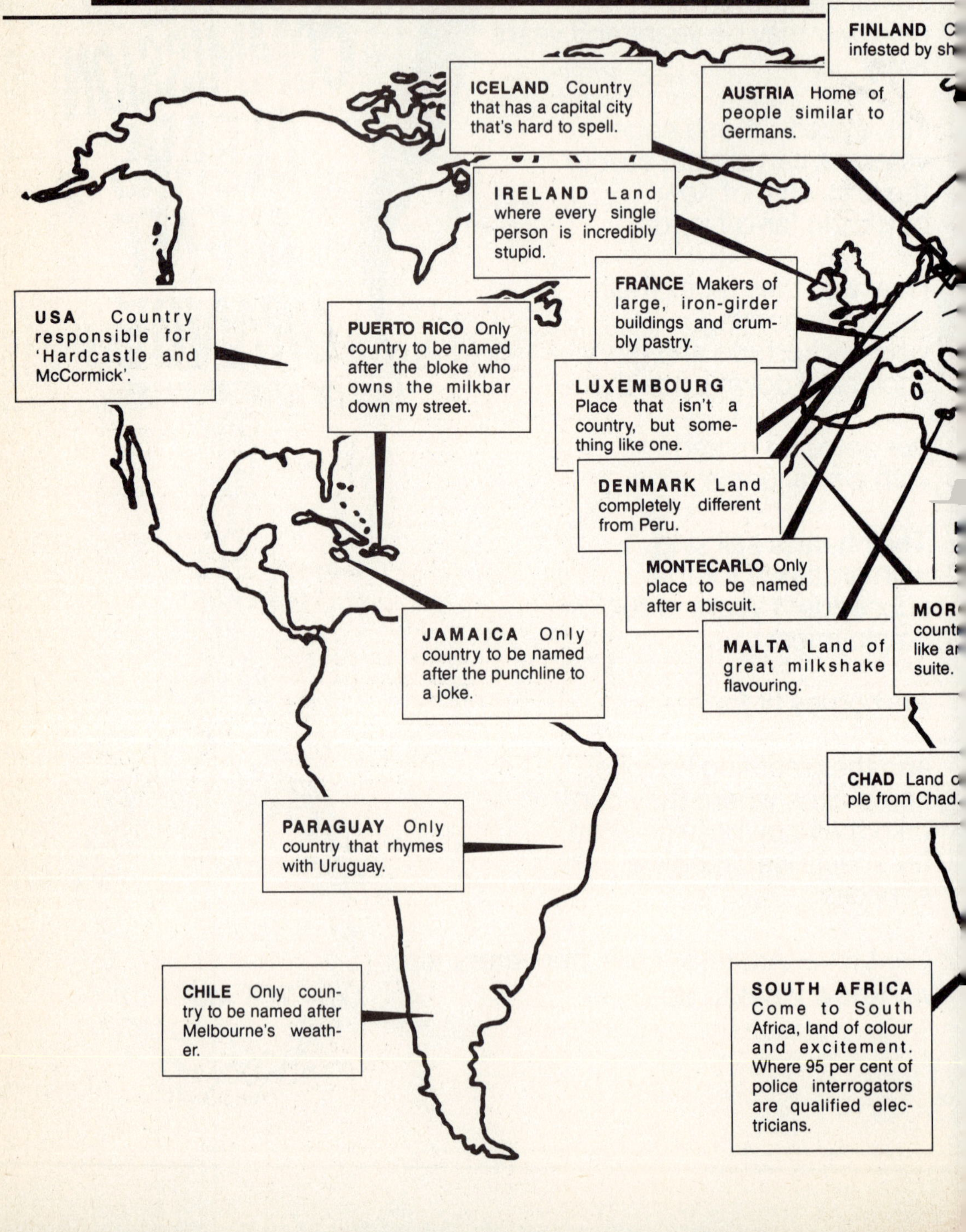

FINLAND C
infested by sh

ICELAND Country that has a capital city that's hard to spell.

AUSTRIA Home of people similar to Germans.

IRELAND Land where every single person is incredibly stupid.

FRANCE Makers of large, iron-girder buildings and crumbly pastry.

USA Country responsible for 'Hardcastle and McCormick'.

PUERTO RICO Only country to be named after the bloke who owns the milkbar down my street.

LUXEMBOURG Place that isn't a country, but something like one.

DENMARK Land completely different from Peru.

MONTECARLO Only place to be named after a biscuit.

MOR
countr
like ar
suite.

JAMAICA Only country to be named after the punchline to a joke.

MALTA Land of great milkshake flavouring.

CHAD Land o
ple from Chad.

PARAGUAY Only country that rhymes with Uruguay.

CHILE Only country to be named after Melbourne's weather.

SOUTH AFRICA Come to South Africa, land of colour and excitement. Where 95 per cent of police interrogators are qualified electricians.

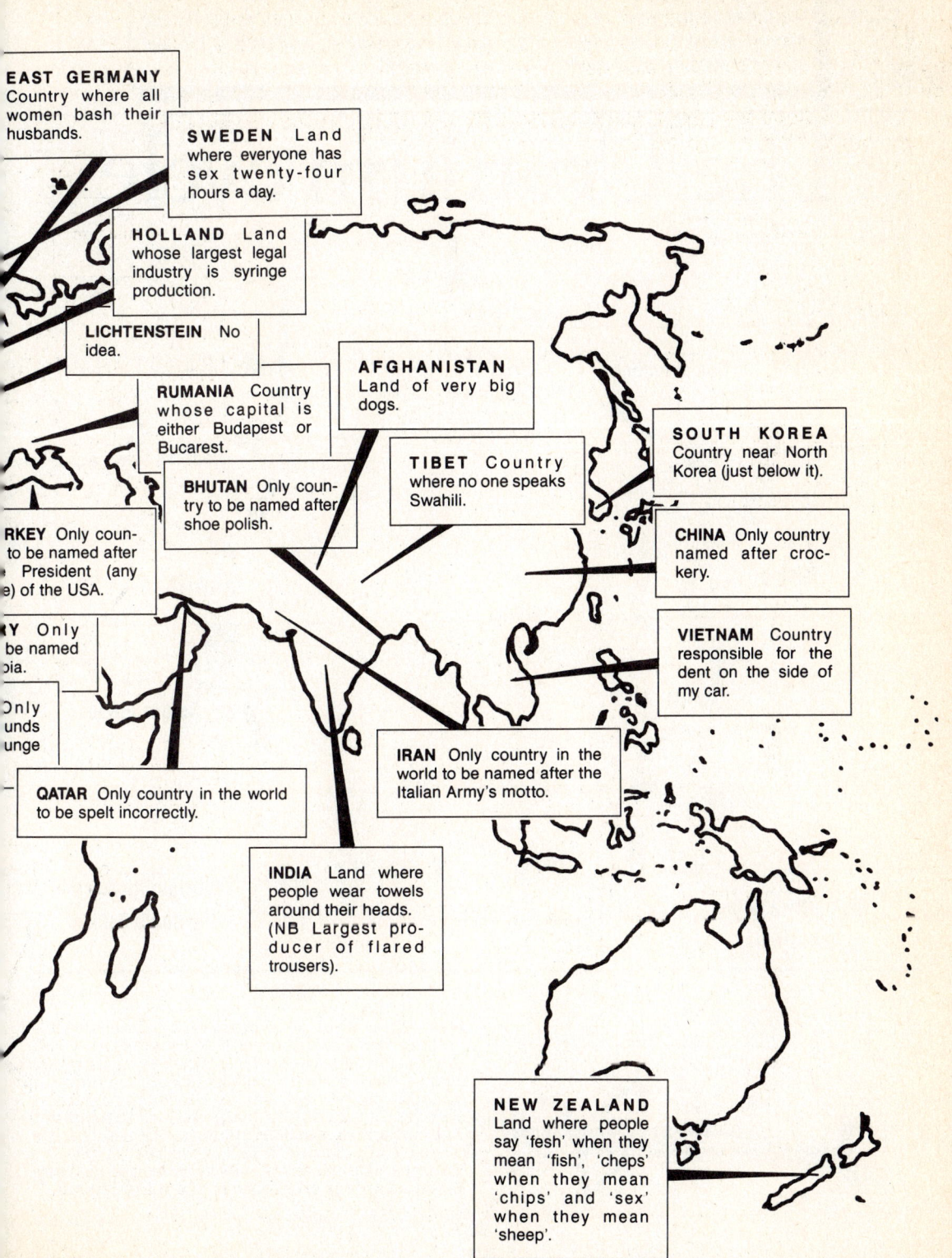

EAST GERMANY Country where all women bash their husbands.

SWEDEN Land where everyone has sex twenty-four hours a day.

HOLLAND Land whose largest legal industry is syringe production.

LICHTENSTEIN No idea.

RUMANIA Country whose capital is either Budapest or Bucarest.

AFGHANISTAN Land of very big dogs.

BHUTAN Only country to be named after shoe polish.

TIBET Country where no one speaks Swahili.

SOUTH KOREA Country near North Korea (just below it).

RKEY Only coun-to be named after President (any e) of the USA.

RY Only be named bia.

CHINA Only country named after croc-kery.

VIETNAM Country responsible for the dent on the side of my car.

Only unds unge

IRAN Only country in the world to be named after the Italian Army's motto.

QATAR Only country in the world to be spelt incorrectly.

INDIA Land where people wear towels around their heads. (NB Largest pro-ducer of flared trousers).

NEW ZEALAND Land where people say 'fesh' when they mean 'fish', 'cheps' when they mean 'chips' and 'sex' when they mean 'sheep'.

COMMANDANT HERBERT BOOTH The Salvation Army leader remembered as founding father of our nation's great film industry. In 1900 he made Soldiers of the Cross, *a two hour religious epic filmed on a Melbourne tennis court. The movie consisted of film, slides and constant evangelical interruptions, a formula still employed by most modern Australian cinemas.*

The Uranium cycle

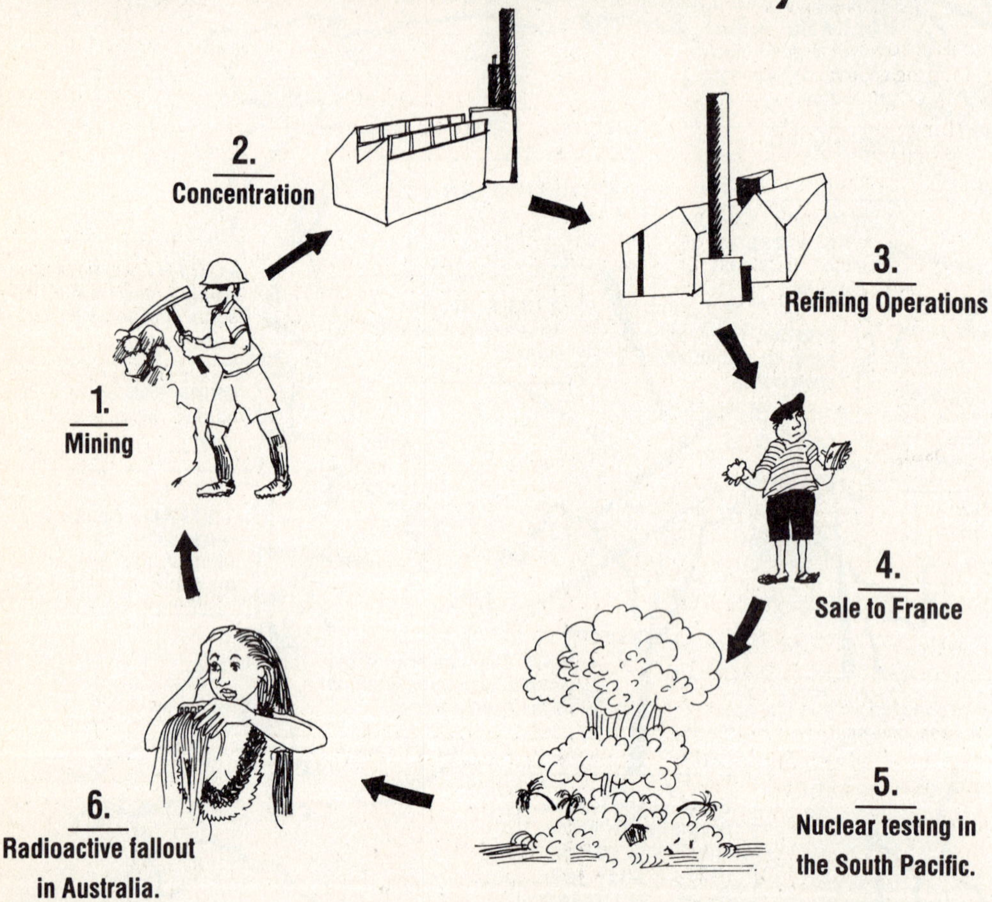

1.
Mining

2.
Concentration

3.
Refining Operations

4.
Sale to France

5.
Nuclear testing in the South Pacific.

6.
Radioactive fallout in Australia.

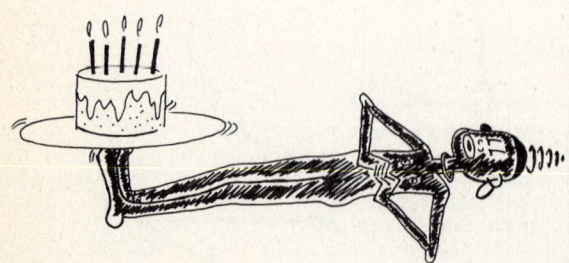

OBITUARY

It is with a great sense of regret that we note the passing of one of this country's finest actors. Geoff 'Mr Sambo' Hughes died last Tuesday, as he would always have wished – performing at a children's birthday party. Geoff had an illustrious career as an actor, appearing in many venues throughout Tasmania and southern Victoria. He reached the pinnacle of his fame in 1978 when the 'Mr Sambo Thumps a Darkie Show' was awarded the national Boma award for excellence in shopping centres.

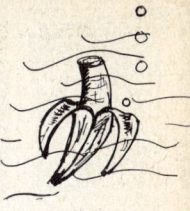

ANNETTE KELLERMAN *Australia's first truly international movie star, Annette was spotted by US producers for her ability to consume a banana underwater. This earned her the title role in a 1914 melodrama* Neptune's Daughter *in which the Aussie actress notched up another world first – appearing nude in a beach scene (without the banana).*

HI HONEY, I'M HOME!
(An essay in comparative American psychology)

American comedy has seen a great deal in the way of brilliance[1]. But few comics have ever come close to the startling originality of America's finest performing ensemble – the Brady Bunch. From the moment Mike and Carol take their six children – the youngest one in curls[2] – and move in together, we know something very special is about to occur. It's the story of a man named Brady, who was bringing up three boys of his own[3]. The Oxford scholar Peter Leet[4] puts it best, 'mysterious, enigmatic, equivocal. Just some of the words I use to impress people . . .'

But we must never forget that the Bradys are a family facing change. Marcia has her teeth straightened,[5] Greg moves into the attic,[6] Jan gets glasses and develops a heroin habit[7]. These are real crises. And yet the comedy raises more questions that it ever answers. Who stole Kitty Carry All[8]? How did Marcia lose her locket[9]? Why can't Carol stop wearing mini-skirts in 1974[10]? Maybe the answer is as Peter Leet[11] himself once suggested, 'poignant, passionate, pronounced, just some of the words that are quite close to each other in the dictionary . . .'

Yet what of the comedy? Was it not Alice who made an artform of overacting and whose monotonous sarcasm lent an edge to every kitchen scene? But she appears only briefly in the title sequence *and* slept with a butcher.[12]

In closing, it is difficult to know how one can sum up the Brady family. As one recent critic[13] put it, they represent America's single greatest argument for birth control. But perhaps I'll let Oxford's best Bradyian scholar, Peter Leet,[14] have the final say, 'harder, slower, wait, sorry. Just some of the words my wife uses during the physical act of love . . .'[15]

1 Chaplin, Keaton, Marx Bros.
2 See Bronowski's discussion of Mike Brady's Afro hair style as evidence of an incestuous link with his youngest daughter *(Works* Vol II).
3 Fienberg stresses the significance of the family dog in his essay 'Alice: socio-sexual role playing vs. the peanut butter and jelly sandwich' (1978).
4 Leet, *Sherwood Schwartz, The Man* (Oxford 1972, p. 345).
5 Brady Bunch, ep. 27.
6 Brady Bunch, ep. 49.
7 See Grossman's excellent treatise 'Jan Brady's Death; Myth or Myopia?'
8 Fienberg, ibid.
9 supra op. cit.
10 Just checking
11 Hardly worth the effort, was it?
12 See S. Cohen's discussion of this relationship, 'Alice & Sam's Ano-Meat Pact'.
13 Bronowski, *loc. cit., supra, ibid, et al.*
14 Leet, 'Peter Brady's Other Funky Pad', (Oxford, 1975).
15 Peter is currently completing a paper on premature ejaculation, in academic circles.

THE JOY OF AUSSIE SEX

'The Workshop'

POSITION 37:

(B-grade Australian actor/actress on bottom, successful producer/director on top.)

This was sent in by Sarah Wilson, aged four.

This finger painting was sent to us by Kylie Adams, aged seven.

And this was sent in by Jane, aged five.

PLEASE, DON'T LEAVE POSTAGE STAMPS
AND ENVELOPES LYING AROUND WHERE
YOUNG CHILDREN CAN FIND THEM.
WE'RE SICK OF THIS CRAP.

Jilly on Love

RONA Jilly. You are a brilliant actress. A woman of so many talents.

JILLY Yeah.

RONA Yet you are prepared to sit here and let me, a personal of almost criminal intensity, ask you a question so convoluted, so banal, it almost defies response. How do you handle that?

JILLY By taking myself *very, very* seriously.

RONA You're a brave woman. I'm now going to lean forward and gently touch you on the knee. How do you deal with that?

JILLY By leaning back and placing a forefinger to my lips. Then changing camera angles.

RONA Jilly, you're a wife and mother now –
JILLY NODS.
I'll do the nodding, if you don't mind.

JILLY Sure.

RONA Tell me, what would you do if I asked you a very personal question about your relationships.

JILLY I'd start to answer by taking in a lot of air. Then I'd pretend not to be able to speak. But in a very heroic way I'll struggle on through the tears and boost my energy just enough to start talking some crap about God

RONA And then I'll cut you off, just when people think we've reached our most asinine depths, because I want the last shot on me.

JILLY Creep.

RONA Bitch.

37

"TREV TALKING"

I was talking with Prowsey the other night over a few ambers and we decided it was time to have a chat with all you blokes out there, one to one. So all you womenfolk go off and make yourselves useful for a couple of minutes. We'll call you when we're done. Off you go, then, bye.

Women, eh? Can't live with 'em, can't live without 'em.

Nah, but seriously, fellas, we just wanna tell ya' how to look after ya' woman; 'cos when it comes down to it, she's the one you have to put up with for the rest of your life. Now the first thing to remember is that to have a successful relationship with your wife, you need the three essential elements; love, respect, and of course, the physical side of marriage – violence.

But what happens then? You're labelled. People come up to ya' and call ya' a wife basher. Well, let us tell ya'. Whenever people come up to us and call us 'wife bashers', it makes . . . it makes us feel . . . proud, real proud. And we're touched by that. Cos we're just average blokes, like every other person in the world. And just like everyone else in the world, we got needs, we got desires – we wanna injure people too.

So that's it, fellas, look after your little lady. And if you really care about her, make sure she's an ambulance subscriber. That's the least she deserves.

Come on darlins! Come back in! Enjoy the rest of the reading. Don't forget, fellas, treat 'em mean, keep 'em keen.

THE JOY OF AUSSIE SEX
'The Pub Squash'

POSITION 46:

(Woman on bottom, mates on top.)

VACANCY female junior for lunchtime and evening work. Good rates for the right girlie. Must be outgoing and obliging (if you know what I mean).
Apply Mr P Branton.

Mr Branton: Oh, this is outrageous, this is unbelievable! Did you or did you not say to Miss Fenton 'Let's make love in the tea-room?'

Ms Feekes: Oh, maybe in passing. Let's not start reading into things.

Mr Branton: Did you use the expression, 'thousand volt love pump?'

Ms Feekes: Oh, this is unbelievable, you can't carry on a normal conversation in an office without some paranoid secretary . . . Yes, I did say that . . . in a very caring and sensitive way.

Mr Branton: (Quoting from file) 'I'm going to shoot you with my passion pistol?'

Ms Feekes: If you're going to keep quoting me . . .

Mr Branton: 'Moisture-seeking missile?'

Ms Feekes: Oh, you take anything out of context and say it coldly like that . . .

Mr Branton: Did you, last week, say to Miss Fenton, that you 'may have something to help her stir the coffee with?'

Ms Feekes: No! Nor was there any reference to 'artificial sweeteners'.

Mr Branton: Listen. Why should I have to sit here and have my integrity, my reputation, questioned by a woman with norks as big as yours?

In some countries they don't have advertising . . .

In some countries, women aren't allowed to drape themselves across the bonnets of cars.
They aren't allowed to mate with chocolate bars.
In some countries, women are actually forbidden to express themselves in wet T-Shirts.
Advertising. You'd probably notice it more if it had a split up the sides.

SIR DOUGLAS MAWSON Australia's most celebrated Antarctic explorer, he once ate his dogs to stay alive. The last animal killed was a husky called Pavlova, given to Mawson personally by Dame Nellie Melba. He ate its paws in a stew.

IVF – A MIRACLE BREAKTHROUGH

Jan Avery talks to the Reynolds couple about the heartache and triumph of infertility.

Gary and Barbara Reynolds are relaxing on a leather lounge suite in their comfortable North Shore home. Now they are able to joke about the traumas of the last two years. However, Barb is quick to point out that there were times when she felt like giving up. Soon after they were married, a routine medical check-up revealed that as a couple they would be infertile.

For eight years, they tried unsuccessfully to have a child. Then, as a final desperate measure, they agreed to sleep together. When this failed they came to the In Vitro Fertilisation Centre in Melbourne.

Barbara Reynolds takes up the story.
'Oh, the staff were absolutely marvellous. And they've agreed to let us both be there, for the decanting.'
For couples like the Reynolds, the IVF programme is their only hope for a family. They explain.

'Well, I did manage one successful pregnancy by natural means, but I slipped coming down some very steep stairs . . . and I lost the baby,' said Barb.
'It just flew out of her hands and we never found it again,' Gary concurred.
For Gary Reynolds, the IVF Programme has changed his life. He was once thought infertile, but with a lot of support, a small test-tube and some very fine Swedish publications, Gary will soon be a father. The child is due in less than two months and the proud parents plan to call it after its mother – 'Pyrex Reynolds.'

THE LATEST IN CAMERA TECHNOLOGY

Presenting the NEW
SUSCHI K177B FULLY AUTO CAMERA

An SLR so advanced, you just can't go wrong!

With the latest in operator warning systems. There's never been a camera like it. Just look at its latest features:

STOP! Too Dark   STOP! Too Blurry   STOP! Too Boring

CHARLES STURT *The popular explorer who claimed to have met a tribe of Aboriginals in Central Australia with intimate knowledge of Freemasonry, giving signs known only to the mystic brotherhood.*

A Letter from the Managing Director

You know, this is just typical. A couple of hypochondriacs drop dead and this company is instantly dragged through the mud. You'll note that all the complaints so far have come from women! Not one male consumer has found anything wrong with our inter-uterine devices. And do you know why? Because they're completely safe. In fact, the bloody things are university tested! (And neither Leanne nor Debbie had any problems.)

But still we get a pile of statistics thrown at us. Sure, 99 per cent of users have suffered major internal injury or death – you get that with any pharmaceutical product. But what about the other 1 per cent? They're probably out there, right now playing volleyball – and winning! Listen. Our products are safe. We surveyed a random group of 200 women and not one complaint. Not a whisper.

(I'd like to take this opportunity to thank the ladies of Our Lady Of Good Hope for their tireless co-operation.)

A SELECTION OF 'CONSAFE' 's PROVEN DEVICES

NEWTON'S SECOND LAW OF MOTION.

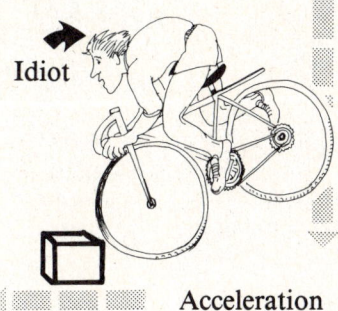

Gravity

Idiot

Acceleration

$$9.8a \pm g =$$

COMPLETE THICKHEAD

THE DOUBLE STANDARD

AUSTRALIA'S LEADING DAILY NEWSPAPER

SPACE PROBE FINDS NO LIFE ON MARS

Inside: Kinder AIDS scare

OBITUARY
TAGBOSH O'REILLY (1937-1987) author, builder, designer, and stonemason. Inspired amateurs all round the world to become builders with his series of owner-builder books, *'Owner-built Homestead', 'The Healthy House',* and *'Vegetarian Verandahs'.*

Wrote about low-cost buildings, the use of natural materials like earth, stone and timber, and the development of skills and self-reliance.

Died 24 February 1987, at 50, when an experimental clay and bamboo dome he built collapsed on him as he slept.

THE MARS DAILY

THE PAPER MORE MARTIANS READ

Strange Gadget Found in Desert

Inside; AIDS Colour Lift-Out

CONSTABLE WILLIAM MURRAY *When an innocent dingo trapper was killed by savage natives in 1928 it was Mounted Constable Murray who led a party of white settlers into Central Australia, shooting dead thirty-one Aboriginal men and women. At the official enquiry, Constable Murray was asked why he took no prisoners. The lanky Australian lawman quipped, 'What use is a wounded blackfella a hundred miles from civilisation?' The enquiry found all the killings had been 'justified'.*

LAND WHITES (A Farce in One Act)

MR LANGLEY   Long time ago, in Dreamtime, Jimmy, whiteman come, build whiteman houses.

MR BARNES   Whiteman stay long, long time. Do you understand, Jimmy?

BOONG   (Nods)

MR BARNES   Good, plenty good!

MR LANGLEY   And so whiteman really own all this land, from big red rock to big blue water. Do you understand?

BOONG   You want to purchase all the freehold estates between Ayers Rock and Darwin?

MR BARNES   Good! Plenty Good!

BOONG   In return for?

MR LANGLEY   Two shiny balls and a magic numbers machine.

BOONG   Two marbles and a digital watch. Tell me, gentlemen, are you proposing a complete divesting of title, or merely some sort of leasehold arrangement?

MR BARNES   . . . two shiny balls and a magic numbers machine . . .

BOONG   I see. Well, thank you for the offer, but . . .

MR BARNES   Er, Jimmy, you're not going walkabout, are you?

BOONG   No, I'm going to my car.

What's Mr Golliwog's South African friend put round his neck? Join the dots to find out.

LAWRENCE *Captain of the Aboriginal cricket team that toured England in February 1868. The team included Bullocky, Dick-a-Dick, King Cole, Shepherd (v.c.), Jim, Two-Penny, Red Cap and Bob Simpson.*

ANZAC DAY 1990

Notice to ALL marchers

Marchers will assemble in the following order for the march down to the Shrine of Remembrance:

8th Light Feminists Refuge Riflery
Women Against Rape in War Armoured Division
22nd Light Dyke Brigade
Women Who Want To Be Women Battalion Collective
Royal Mounted Lesbian Separatists
Corp. C. Perkin (aged 84): last surviving Anzac and alleged pack rapist
Women Who Want To Be First in Line

Lest we forget . . .
Creche facilities will be provided, as well as latrines (comfort stations) en route.

25/7/86
GUTTER IN BRUNSWICK ST. VIC

Dear Malcolm,
How are you? Well, I hope. I'm O.K. They reckon they've got my leprosy under control. My eldest died yesterday, but the police assure me they'll get onto it as soon as they can.
Anyway, I just wanted to say good on you for all the work you're doing for the blacks in South Africa. It's good to see you taking you're life-long crusade for black rights 2000 miles from our shores, where they really need it. I mean, I was shocked to hear that in that country, the black people are actually beaten by police and in some cases detained illegally in jails.
You're a ripper bloke, Mal. After all the great work you've done for us black brothers here, we're proud to see that you're showing the whole world how concerned Australians are about Racism.

P.S. You must have alot of guts.

In some countries they don't have advertising
In some countries people are thrown into stinking, rat-infested sewers every day. In fact I've got this friend, Marjorie Godsnell, and she went to Eritrea and she was bombed, raped and force-fed dung beetles for two months and she *swears* they didn't have advertising.
Advertising – you'd probably notice it more if it was worth watching . . .

What I like about Australia is the blacks. I think they're great. Everyone should have one.'
National Party Policy Statement

THE GRAMMARIAN

OFFICIAL NEWSPAPER OF PENTHORN GRAMMAR SCHOOL
EDITOR: R. MURDOCH (2B)

Mothers' Club In Wife-Swapping Sex Orgy Row!!!

The President of Penthorn's Mothers' Club, Mrs Betty MacGregor, yesterday announced there would be changes to the tuckshop roster due to next Thursday's half-holiday.

Headmistress In Shock Porn Drug Ring!!!

The Headmistress of Penthorn Grammar, Mrs C. Cullen, 107, has complained about the large number of boys smoking in the toilets. 'If it does not cease,' said the attractive mother of 3, at her weekly assembly, 'detentions may be handed out.'

Sportmaster's Anal Sex Disgrace!!!

Penthorn's long-serving sportsmaster, Mr Barry Cranton, announced there would be no football training today. 'After so much rain,' said the colloquial coach, 'the ground's completely buggered.'

Chapel Desecrated In Black Mass Ritual!!!

The school chaplain would like to remind all students that prayer books are to be neatly stacked at the back of each pew after morning service.

Drama

The Drama Society, led by Mr Storrock, is to be commended for another fine production this year. Few will forget Jacinta Storrock's moving rendition of Portia's main soliloquy from the *The Merchant of Venice,* unusual as it was appearing halfway through a performance of *The Sound of Music.* However, the musical provided a timely change of direction after the tragedy of last year's *Julius Caesar* when Brutus (Nic Spanos) and a masked centurion ('Chooker' Hughes) allowed personal friction to interfere with their performances. Mr Storrock wisely kept all action props out of this year's production.

Talks

* Miss E. Hampton gave an excellent talk on contraception which proved of great interest to all who attended, and may hopefully offset the growing demand for creche facilities in the middle school.
* Last years' school captain, Darren Derby, delivered a fascinating talk on Long Bay Gaol. Darren holds a secure position in the prison's laundry, and should be an inspiration to all the Penthonian final years. Special thanks to the eight armed guards who helped make this excellent Careers Night Talk possible.

JOHN FERRES The English migrant who arrived in Melbourne in 1848 to become manager of that city's intellectual evening newspaper the Herald. John was the first to introduce a steam printing machine to the colonies and, later, weekly bingo games to the front pages.

Death

It was with great sense of loss that Penthorn recorded the death of Jeff 'Dicko' Bradley, early this year. A student of some five years, 'Dicko' was respected and feared by all who knew him. Quite frankly, the kid was a prick. Loud, aggressive, and overbearingly stupid, Dicko was your classic schoolboy bully – on his own, a complete wimp, but surrounded by henchmen (never 'friends') he would turn into a viscious little thug. In class he was a complete gumboot and we only let him into Penthorn because the oaf could drop punt the leather seventy metres. Oh God, I'm glad he's finally dead; we'll probably declare the anniversary a school holiday and make the truck driver an honorary Old Boy. Our deepest sympathy to his family and loved ones in this time of grief.

Sports Report

This year has proved very exciting for Penthorn, with the soccer team doing well, and the introduction of Australian Rules providing a choice of winter sports. A crisis loomed over the availability of training grounds when the council bulldozed the local tip, but some consolation was found in the drop of typhoid cases reported by Matron. There was an unfortunate all-in brawl during the cricket final, and I must take this opportunity to again reprimand those Penthonians involved; the Catholic boys were here as our guests, and there was absolutely no justification for Malcolm McLeish and Co. urinating on their oranges.

Missing

Once again, our school bursar asks your help in locating these old Penthonians who have gone 'missing' from our Old Boys Address Register. Last known addresses are:

R. Trimbole (Spain? Ireland?)
R. Biggs (Rio)
M. Farqhar (NSW Magistrates Court)
A. Eichmann (Israel)

Virgin's Naked Football Romp

After a slow start to the season, Penthorn's first XVIII had a glorious victory last Saturday, defeating Bridgestone Methodist Ladies College. The match followed a mix-up of venues which saw our top footballers go up against Bridgestone's Junior Girls Debating Team. On the topic, 'That Might Makes Right,' Penthorn won easily by six goals, despite several members being sent off for eye-gouging and a very bad score for presentation from two of the judges.

Finance Report

(By R. Holmes a Court, Jnr)
Trading was quite fierce today in the school tuckshop with jam donuts and cheese twisties both closing at 30¢. Health foods again took a tumble, with salad rolls being marked back 10¢ before trading closed at the end of lunchtime. The All Tasties Index finished at 1734.4 up 11.4, no doubt reflecting the release of favorable Real Pocket Money Purchase Power Figures at recess today.

After his unsuccessful takeover bid last week, playground bully, Sandros Donatis, has been made the subject of an official inquiry into allegations of unfair trading. It appears that Mr Donatis has been offering unopened packets of Sherbet Whiz Fizz in return for certain Footy Swap Cards, throwing the tuckshop into a liquidity freeze. The hearing will be held outside the Staff Room after school tonight by Economics teacher Mr Dittnel. Preliminary profit report for the Tuckshop predicts a profit rise of 15 per cent reflecting strong sales of the new cigarette and beer division.

PHAR LAP *Like so many of our great Aussie heroes, Phar Lap was born in New Zealand. A stunning racehorse, Phar Lap summed up the hopes and dreams of a young nation, being killed in America and stuffed by the Australian Government.*

Chunda

TOURS PRESENT . . .
NEW ZEALAND on twenty pesos a day!!!

Geoff, 24 (National-bankteller)

Geoff, 24
'Chunda Tours gave me two beer-filled weeks of ragin' all day on a bus, and falling asleep each night in my own vomit. Unreal.'

Chunda Tours have been successfully operating coach tours of New Zealand since early last week. Our philosphy is to pack as many lonely young people into a bus as possible and make sure the toilets clog up just outside of Auckland. We invite you to broaden your horizons, learn about new cultures and see the boongs over here in New Zealand. Chunda offers three (3) categories of coach tour: SUPERIOR (with toilet), DELUXE (with indoor toilet), and ECONOMY (fitted plastic pants). All prices are fully inclusive, except for lunches, transport, accommodation and all sightseeing. So if you're between 18 and 35, and completely lacking in social skills, join our great guys and gals for the trip of a lifetime. (Chunda is an Australian Aboriginal word meaning 'Sacrifice on the bus'). Book now and receive free (3) your complete Chunda Tour kit, including maps, compass and a spacious, distinctively styled Chunda travel bag, so you can look like a galah wherever you go.

Seeing the sights of New Zealand!

Your Chunda hostess will haunt you for the duration of your stay . . .

CHUNDA'S WELCOME: on arrival in Auckland or Christchurch (depending on strike action) your local Chunda hostess will be on hand to welcome you. She will haunt you for the duration of your stay.

At the completion of your first day's touring we invite you to join us for a pre-dinner Happy hour, with complimentary drinks on Chunda.

CHUNDA'S MEALS: the great thing about New Zealand (apart from the nasal sex)is that you don't have to adjust to a different style of cuisine than that which you so enjoy at home. No greasy wog food on either island!

FRINGE BENEFITS: as we tour the majestic landscape that is New Zealand you'll be invited to share in an ancient Kiwi custom – registering for the dole at every CES branch under a different name.

So come on! Here's your chance to spend two (3) weeks on the road with a busload of bank employees on annual leave.

Here's what people say about Chunda Tours:

Keith, 23
'Taking two weeks off from the bank was the best thing I ever did. I never realised there were so many people with such interesting lumber-jackets before.'

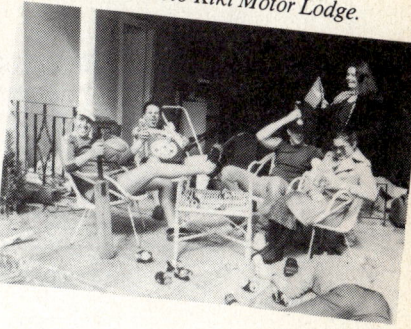

Relaxing in the beer garden of the prestigious Roto-Kiki Motor Lodge.

Chunda's free travel bag!

Karen, 19, (Westpac-customer relations.)

Relaxin' with the boys.

Graeme, 25 (A.N.Z. Junior Branch Manager)

Graeme, 25
'Mate. I've been to Great Keppel, I've chucked in every hotel in Surfers, I never realised there was another place I could inflict cultural damage on!'

Karen, 19
I reckon New Zealand is the best country in the whole of Oceania, after Australia.'

CHUNDA TOURS – WE'LL PROMISE YOU A HOLIDAY YOU'LL NEVER REMEMBER

. . .

DAME JEAN MACNAMARA It was as a result of one woman's lobbying that the great rabbit disease myxomatosis was first introduced into Australia. A viral disease, 'myxo' causes large tumours to form in the connective tissues of a rabbit's skin, especially round the eyes and mouth, closing them after a few days. Many Australians will recall, the humorous sight of these pus-faced vermin careering blindly into trees during the several weeks it takes them to die.

BUM-PER JOKERS!!!

Who says Aussies don't have a sense of humour? Our photographer snapped these mirthful messages on cars and trucks all round the country!

Welders Have Big Dicks

Old Golfers Never Die . . . They Just Lose Their Testes

Brickies Make The Best Bricklayers

Mountain Men Love Having Sexual Intercourse With Women

I  Sex

Electricians Have Huge Throbbing Fuses!!!

I 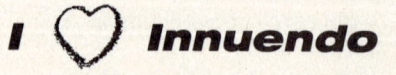 Innuendo

Love Is . . . An Obscure Breed Of Dog

Love Is . . . 'A Metaphysical Construct Imposed On Altruism' — Plato

How To Be A Comedian (by Bruce Goodluck, MLA, Tas)

1/ Get a funny hat
2/ Tell a funny joke

History Fact

The first joke was invented over 500 million years ago. Scientists discovered this by carbon dating the fossilised remains of a bubble gum wrapper.

My name is Henny Bill,
And I'm a very funny lass,
I like to have nude men on stage,
And pinch them on the arse.

I like their nice firm buttocks,
I like their pert wee breasts,
And I like to dance in high heels,
Across their hairy chests.

Oh my name is Henny Bill,
And I'm making lots of money,
Which is the biggest joke of all,
'Cos I'm not even funny.

Hi, I'm a straightman. It's my function in this book to be a sort of foil for the other funny characters. I'm usually a woman or a fairly bland-looking bloke, and I'm just the sort of person you'd expect to be given six lines without an even remotely funny ending.

From a newspaper article: 'Today is a day of Total Fire Ban.'
Seen on the back of a toilet door: 'I hate wogs.'

'LAUGHTER – THE BEST MEDICINE'

The after-dinner speaker was just about to propose a toast to an important gathering of guests, when he slipped, cracking his head open on the podium.
B. Nettlemore, *More Great Jokes*

The bankrobber shoved a note at the pretty teller, reading 'Put the Mony in this bag or else'. The teller read his note, added a message of her own and shoved it back. Her message read, 'you mispelt "money" '. The bank robber shot her in the head, escaping with a large sum of money in a brown Valiant.
C. Cradock, Crow's Nest, NSW

Supreme Court of Victoria

R.v. Giberaldi

Full Court

22 June 1986

Police offences – obscene publications – 'Obscene' – meaning of – expert evidence – finding by magistrate photos obscene and unduly emphasised matters of – 'sex' – meaning of.–

F. Cardonni for the defendant, to move the order absolute (deny everything) W. Astley-Smythe for the informant, to show cause (earn $20,000).

Smith J. The defendant was apprehended by police on the 12th of June for driving an orange Monaro in a built-up area. A subsequent search of his vehicle revealed 2,000 copies of a publication entitled *Backdoor Bazooka Bliss';* this magazine featured photographs of young ladies in various stages of undress. At a preliminary hearing the magistrate found the publication 'obscene' within the meaning of the *Stick Magazine Amendment Act* 1958 (Vic). He relied on the definition of obscene as being 'against the prevailing standards of the community.' Counsel for Mr Giberaldi appealed, arguing that photos of naked women being subjected to acts of gratuitous sexual violence are completely in keeping with prevailing community standards. The Court accepts this contention.

Turning to the accompanying text, there is, however, some division. My learned colleague Barker J. felt that though the word 'throbbing' on its own may not tend to deprave and corrupt, the phrase 'throbbing 50 volt love pump' may indeed do so.

Asquith J. dissented, stating that using terms such as 'thunder plunderer' or the aforementioned term, does not constitute obscenity as, say 'big red love missile' does, and cannot be contrued as obscene. Although he accepted that 'blue-veined junket pumping' could be construed thus, and suggested that this be changed in further publications to 'bonking'.

The hearing then centred its attention on whether 'fast shooting passion pistol' (on page 22) constituted a breach of the *Act*. The Bench agreed that it did, though they concurred that 'jism juice injector' did not. The entire Bench liked 'slamming sausage stuffer', especially Oakley J. who retired last week. We wish him well.

As a final point, counsel for the defendant argued that as the magazines were locked in Mr Giberaldi's boot, they could not deprave and corrupt. Asquith J. accepted this in part, and complimented counsel on his dress sense. He quoted the judgement of Lord Sands in *Carter v Taylor* (1931 S.C. (J) 10, 'Put it away, Mr Taylor, you'll only embarass yourself.'

In the view of the defendant's previous good record, and his undertaking to leave book publishing and enter the furniture warehouse trade, the court is prepared to let him off with a warning: always check your tyre pressure before a long journey.

Baker J.: I agree.

Asquith J.: Me too.

Oakley J.: Could I look at p.22 again?

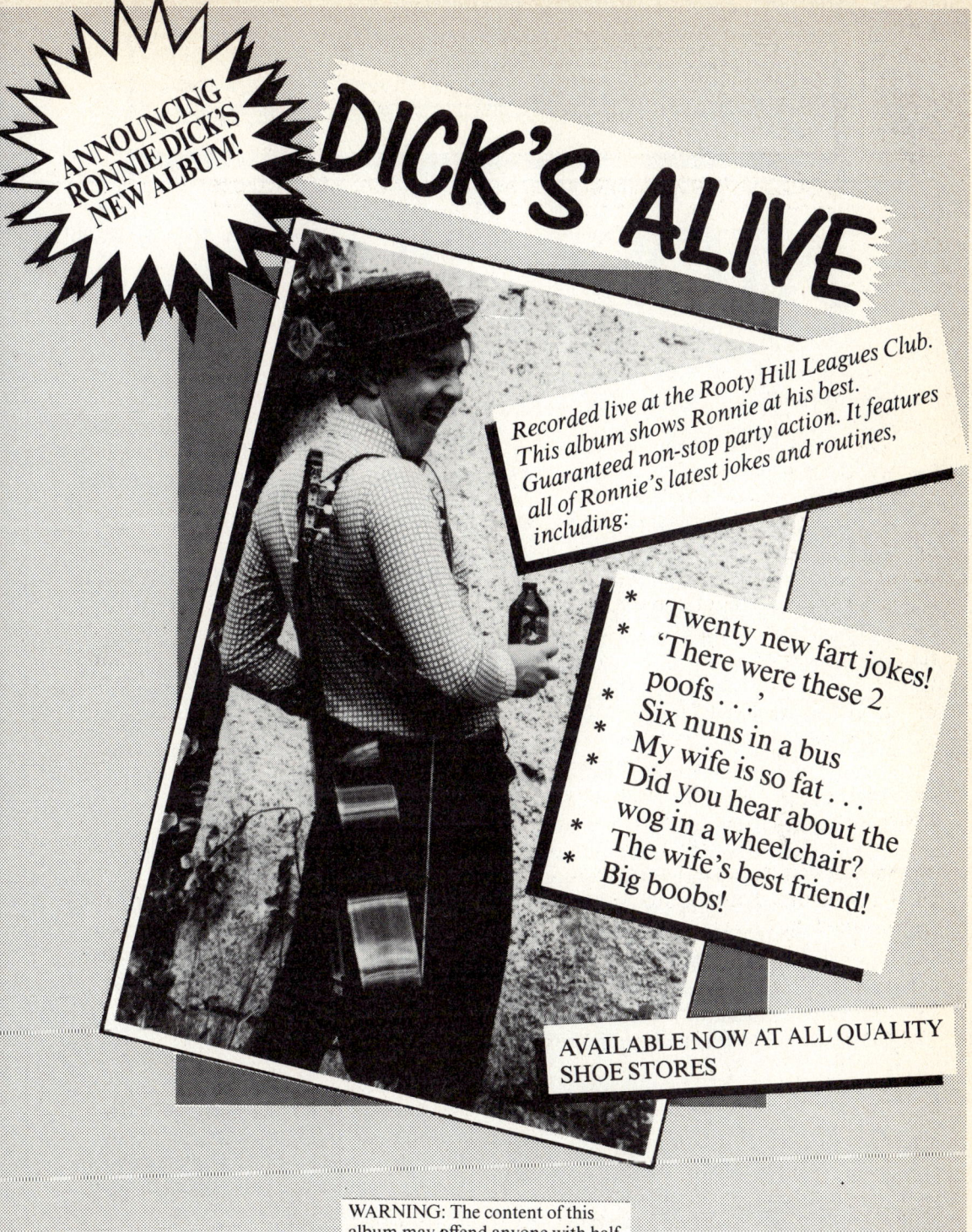

AIDS

NO-NONSENSE AND OBJECTIVE FACTS ABOUT THE KILLER DISEASE

– From the Festival of Light

Traces of the AIDS virus have been found in saliva. There is also clear evidence that the virus has been transmitted through sweat, casual contact, swimming pools, mosquitoes, touching crockery used by an AIDS sufferer and even walking past the house of someone carrying the virus and waving. There is also preliminary evidence that thinking of an AIDS victim can cause transmission. Studies on the infectivity of reading AIDS related material have yet to be released, however a preliminary report concludes that the article must be over 300 words (not counting notes).

Scientific research concludes that there is only one sure way to successfully eradicate the killer virus. All countries must join together and, in a very loving and Christian manner, systematically kill all practising homosexual men.

MERELY MALE

A light-hearted look at our weaker sex!

FLOORED!
Last week after a particularly heavy session at the pub, MM (aggressive husband) came home and broke my jaw in two places for burning his tea. When I lapsed into a coma, he said, 'Get up, you stupid bitch!!!'
Ms B. Cullen,
Perth Women's Refuge
(THIS LETTER WINS $10!)

CAPSIZE!
A funny thing happened last night. MM (quadriplegic son) went to go outside not realising someone had removed the wheelchair ramp from our back steps. When I got outside he was lying on his back in a puddle!
Mrs P. Brantell,
Newcastle

QUESTIONS?
Little eight-year-old madame was helping MM (father) paint our back fence when she asked, 'Where do fairies come from?' MM replied, 'Shut up and get me a rag!'
Mrs. R. Taylor,
Pembroke

CROSS TO BEAR
My husband and I have been devout Catholics all our lives. Last year during the Papal visit, MM (the Pope) turned up twenty minutes late to his open-air mass. We have since sold our Holden.
Eileen O'Shea (Mrs)
Qld

Aunt Martha's Problem Page

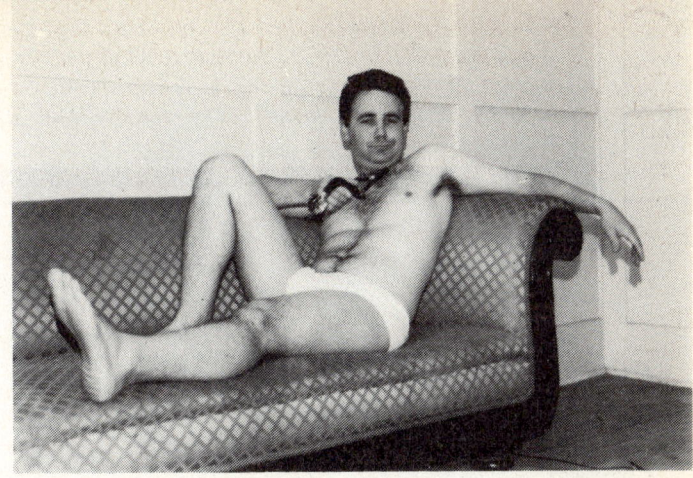

PAINFUL DISCHARGE

For several months now, I have been experiencing a painful brownish discharge. It is particularly noticeable when I exercise. I recently stopped taking the pill after two years. Could this have anything to do with it?

— Susan, 18

The Hydrangea is a very hardy plant and will thrive almost anywhere. However, I suggest a shaded location, and use lime and chemical fertilizers sparingly.

PREGNANT?

Several people have told me that you can get pregnant from sitting on a bottle that others have recently drunk from. Is this true?

— Julie, 23

Yes.

INCEST

A few weeks ago something happened that upset me very much. I was lying in bed, almost asleep, when I heard my father come in. He lent over, tucked my bedclothes in, and whispered 'goodnight'. Then he left. I have been too scared to tell my mother for fear of what might happen. Is my father sick?

— Katrina, 14

Yes. Your father is a twisted, perverted old man who should be immediately reported to the authorities and castrated.

MORAL DILEMMA

I am a strict Catholic and naturally don't believe in the pill or any other form of artificial contraception as being against the natural will of God and the sacred edicts of my Church. However, I like sleeping with most guys I meet. What should I do?

— Angela, 17

Become a Methodist?

For today's natural woman, a fragrance that says the things you want to say about life. Wild, exotic, like wind in your hair . . .

Flatulénce

'Flatulénce. It's me, maybe it's you too? . . . No, it's me . . .

Mike's Clito Quiz!
HOW MUCH DO YOU LIKE SEX?

1 **How often do you have sex?**
Hourly?
Monthly?
Anally?
Whenever Allan Border makes a century?

2 **When you have sex, what do you think of?**
Your guy?
What you're going to wear tomorrow?
The loss of circulation in your arm?
Allan Border making a ton?

3 **When you think of Allan Border making a ton, do you:**
Orgasm?
Laugh hysterically?

4 **When your guy comes do you:**
Get undressed?
Look surprised?
Tell him he's improving?
Answer the door?

SIR ROBERT MENZIES *Perhaps Australia's best-loved PM, it was Sir Robert who first allowed British atomic testing in this country, assuring the public that it was completely safe. Between 1952-57 we played proud host to a total of twelve separate explosions, including the unforgettable England-Australia tests at Maralinga.*

Professor A.T. Philane
Chairman,
Dept. Nuclear Physics
ANU
Canberra ACT

A.M. Craddock
Managing Director
Nuclear Development Co.
Sydney

Dear Mr Craddock,

When I was first asked to design a nuclear reactor for use under the Sydney Opera House, I went home, and looked at my wife and children, and thought long and hard about the implications of such a concept. In the end, I decided that any such project would constitute the greatest act of short-sighted lunacy one could possibly be capable of. In short, it would pose the gravest threat, not just to ourselves, but to our kids and all further generations. As an Australian scientist, and a member of the world scientific community, I would like your firm to record my complete and unequivocal rejection of the scheme, both in your records and as a public statement.

Yours
Professor A.T. Philane

PS Plans are on the back. I've placed the main core under the Arts Complex, with the radioactive waste sort of sluicing off into the harbour. Would you please detach this PS, and send my cheque to the Swiss address below.

And now, an apology from the United States.

It is with great regret that I, on behalf of the American people, apologise for everything we've done to the world.

For wearing these clothes we're sorry.

For shouting in public we're also sorry.

We apologise for going woo woo, whenever a cute little black kid with kidney problems comes on the TV.

We apologise for electing a senile, washed-up actor as president . . . twice.

Sorry for shooting him . . . and missing.

We'd also like to apologise for the following:

Magnum P.I.

The Dukes of Hazzard.

Scarecrow & Mrs King.

The A-Team (I like them).

To the following countries we extend our sincerest apologies: Korea, Vietnam, Nicaragua, Grenada and, in the near future, New Zealand.

WOOLLONGONG – THE DAY AFTER

JANE   On the 2nd February of this year, a nuclear strike from the United States wiped out Woollongong. The US has apologised but the facts surrounding it are a little unclear. Today we're fortunate to have Senator Simmons, Minister for Aborigines, the Arts and other National Disasters and David Emery, spokesman for the Reagan Government on Warmth and Understanding.

Senator Simmons, the Australian Government must be deeply concerned.

SENATOR   Very deeply concerned, extremely concerned, almost angry, not with the US mind you, just with the senseless futility of it all.

DAVID   Let me say from the outset that what we are talking about here is a small nuclear accident; fifty, maybe sixty mega-deaths, tops. Most of the scaremongering around has been totally based on fact.

SENATOR   You've as much chance of being killed on the roads as being vaporised in a thermo-nuclear blast.

DAVID   Sure, what's the road toll downunder . . . fifty thousand a year?

JANE   No, seven hundred.

DAVID   In rough terms, it compares favourably. The major objection, as I see it, is that it's a very concentrated form of devastation, and that's a fair comment.

JANE   David, it was a grave mistake. Off the record, on national television, could you tell us how it happened?

DAVID   It seems at this stage, Jane, to have been a typographical error in the secretaries' pool. Two lunch orders of ham-on-rye were misread: Red-Alert, Attack.

JANE   Has there been any form of inquiry?

DAVID   Look, this isn't the time for witch hunts, but the person involved was spoken to quite sharply.

JANE   Let's come back to Woollongong – I refer to it's existence loosely. David, there have been complaints.

DAVID   Yes, it's a cause for some concern to my government, Jane. I think it's an historical hangover, the spectre of Hiroshima etc – people have memories like elephants. Mind you, we got a lot of very positive mail after Nagasaki, and it hasn't stopped. People *still* remember it!

SENATOR   Sure, there's huge devastation and death, you get that with any major catastrophe.

DAVID   Absolutely.

SENATOR   I think it's dangerous – in fact, irresponsible – for the opposition to start slinging mud on this one. If we don't watch our step there's a very real chance of harming the alliance.

DAVID   No, no, that could never happen. We need you.

THE JOY OF AUSSIE SEX
'The Right Royal Rape'

POSITION 64:

(Conservative Australian Prime Minister on bottom, British monarchy on top.)

LANGLEY GEORGE HANCOCK One of Australia's richest and most successful mining magnates, Lang began his career with an asbestos mine in Western Australia, the same place many of his workers ended theirs. Lang is quoted as saying that 'the greed of capitalism is the only driving force there is'.

The Chairman's address at the Annual General Meeting

Dear Shareholders,

    I am very pleased to inform you that 1986-7 has been a very successful year for the Southern Cross Tobacco Co. Despite some opposition from the idiot fringe of the community, this year saw a growth in the total amount of tobacco sold and a steady return on the company's assets.

    It has also seen a growth of ill-informed, unfounded comment about the company's products. No doubt this led to a decrease in the use of tobacco in certain sections of the community. Research has identified these groups as

1 Young pregnant mothers

2 Suffers of emphysema and asthma

3 Lung cancer victims

4 Health freaks and vegetarians

5 Children.

    This Company is not prepared to stand still in the face of this kind of attack and is currently planning an aggressive marketing push, which will include stepping up advertising in hospitals, schools and health shops.

    In addition our public relations department (well, two shielas in hot pants) will tour schools to give talks and hand out samples.

    This year has seen many successes including the liberal use of lobby money to enable some of the more dogmatic potiticians to see it our way. Perhaps the best result was the sales figures from our new cigarette, 'True Blue Fags' and the slogan, 'You wouldn't be fair dinkum without 'em'.

    We hope that our sponsorship of tennis will have similar results. Especially the idea that the players smoke cigarettes in between games. And so, until our meeting next year.

Yours

Sir Samuel Trainer (Hon. Chairman of Pro-Cancer Council of Vic.)

CURRENCY RATES

	BUY SELL		
Q'SLAND YEN	94.8 92.3	SA Rand	You're kidding
US DOL	1.66 1.63		
ARGENT' $D	See wallpaper adv.	UK £	A LOT TOO MUCH

56

$2

$20

TREASURER'S REPORT

From Mr Keating, B. Ec(Hons) Pty Ltd

The PM unveiled his new economic policy to us all this week. It involves a complex scheme of capital redistribution from the upper quartiles of our primary sector towards lower income brackets. Or as he put it, 'We take from the rich, and give to the poor'. We all agreed the proposal was basically sound and that it was only the word 'give' in section 2 that seemed to jar. I suggested the word 'loan' instead and agreed the whole bill could be rushed through both houses in time for the Spring Racing Carnival. After lunch, the Centre Left moved a small amendment – that we 'kill the rich and maim the poor', but we've already got into enough trouble for stealing Liberal policies. Little John Howard would have us for breakfast. Which reminds me, have we taxed them yet? Maybe some sort of Fibre Benefits Levy; a logbook beside every toilet. Must talk it over with Robin . . .

In some countries they don't have advertising . . .

They don't have all those sixty-second breaks in programming, giving you time to make the coffee or go to the bathroom. No, in some countries they let people's bladders explode every ratings period.

Advertising – you'd probably get cystitis without it.

Letter to Australian Youth from the Governor-General

Dear Youth,

As you will no doubt know by now, the Government has done more than any other to make sure that young people have a future in this country. Unfortunately it has failed, and all Australian's under 25 without jobs by 20 June will be deported to New Zealand.

It is a shame which we very much regret. It's not your fault, it's ours, but it's just one of those things. I guess you could call it bad luck; well, rotten luck. It's like when you get blamed for something your sister did. Look, we're in a mess, in fact we're getting shat on, and you hanging around isn't going to help at all. So come on, let's not fiddle about.

You'll be pleased to know that the Cabinet deeply regret the decisions that caused this hiccup in the economy, and you go with their best wishes.

You may ask, 'can we come back if conditions improve?' Now that's a good question, and it makes me believe that we're letting out some bright young minds. The answer is, no. Let's face it, you had a chance to get a haircut and you didn't.

Yours Sincerely

Ninian xxx

'As a Liberal voter, I believe in the mining of uranium, the floating of the dollar, and the introduction of foreign banks.'

'As a Labor voter, I believe in the mining of uranium, the floating of the dollar and the introduction of foreign banks. I further believe that the policies of the Liberal government are utter madness and will ultimately destroy this country.'

A WORD A DAY

'The economy was STUFFED'

Does this mean it was:
– ruined?
– seasonally depressed?
– all the fault of previous Liberal Mismanagement?

ANS: Stuffed (from the Greek 'Keatos')

BANK

PRIORITY ONE

SOME YOUNG AUSTRALIANS TALK ABOUT BEING UNEMPLOYED

'It's great' – **Geoff** (Auckland), currently on the dole under twelve different names.

'I reckon the worst thing about being unemployed is not having a job' – **Greg** (Cairns)

'Sometimes ya' go to an interview right, and ya' can tell that he doesn't like ya', just because of the way ya' talk and spit in the ashtray' – **Brian** (Newcastle)

'As a woman I find it terrible when an interviewer just sits there undressing you with his eyes. Then he dresses you again in the wrong clothes' – **Trish** (Bondi)

'My Dad reckons I should join the army and learn a trade like he did. But there's just not much call for killing women and children these days' – **John** (Balwyn)

'As a woman, I'd like to see government funding for a study to investigate the link between filling out dole forms and toxic shock syndrome.' – **Jenny** (Balmain)

'I used to just sit around all day waitin' for the phone to ring.' And me Mum would say, "Go find a job", so I'd go out wrecking places and bashing people up. That's when the police picked me up. I'll be a sergeant in two weeks' – **Frank** (Fremantle)

The Government's Priority 1 scheme means that young Australians will now be seen, heard, educated, encouraged, fed, watered, and treated as the future of this country. And still not have a job.

SLIM DUSTY Australia's foremost Country and Western performer. Slim's albums include 'Slim Dusty Live at Tamworth', 'Cattle Clump Corner', and the enigmatic 'Songs in the Saddle'.

LEARN TO WRITE COUNTRY MUSIC CORRESPONDENCE COURSE

2nd Term Assignment — *Quite a good effort, much better than your last, "Teenage Heartbreak at the Suicide Jamboree". I feel however that a few changes could have been made and I've outlined them below.*

Look Both Ways

Well he was drivin' home comin' down the
hill on highway 51 — *nice!*
He'd been out whorin', drinkin', gamblin' and
havin' fun
A man's a man he has a choice to guide him
all his days
but before a man decides he better look both
ways.
When you're truckin through life's — *good start.*
intersection
don't forget to pause — *V. Good*
'cos the devil could be comin' through . . .
In a bigger rig than yours.
He had a wife Charlene's her name
she was his pride and joy) *V. Good names*
she looked after Jimmy)
That was his crippled boy — *basic mistake*
and in his house lived his — *should be "shack".*
blind child a heroine unsung
and he even had a cat — *Dog's are far better. More emotion etc trusty you know*
It was in an iron lung — *A bit subtle*
and as he left them all at home
on that fateful day
his wife 'called' out the door to him — *'hollered'*
'Baby, look both ways' — *Never use 'ing', always 'in'. A slip like this could fail you.*
look both ways
When you're trucking through life's
intersection
don't forget to pause.
'cos the devil may be comin' through
In a bigger rig than yours. Look both ways
Look both ways — *Spot on!*
Look both ways

It wasn't hard to see the house // *needs a yonder or something*
at the bottom of the hill
And as he got down closer
He could see it better still.
Me and Jimmy and blind girl Peg — *Why not Peggie-Sue.*
and little Jake the cat — *Great name, pity its a cat.*
were sittin' in the loungeroom
he remembered seeing that
Till his eyes were clouded over
with the sweat that tension makes
when you're steppin' on the pedal . . .
but haven't got no brakes.
Well the truck came through the front door
and knocked Wayne's wheelchair flat — *It may make it more diff to rythme, but peggie-Sue w—*
It crushed the kitten and blind Peg
he loved that goddam cat.
But as he hit the children's beds,
he heard them in a daze, cry out Mummy, — *have be*
Look it's Daddy, he forgot to look both ways. — *be*
When you're truckin through life's
intersection — *thats just carelessness.*
don't forget to pause
'cos the devil may be comin' through
In a bigger rig than yours.
Look both ways. — *'ing', never use 'ing', always 'in'. A slip like that could fail you.*
Look both ways.

CARLTON COWBOYS

One night we were a cruisin'
Alone in Lygon Street
Lookin' for a woman
Or some take-away fries to eat.
We spied a single girl
And screamed
'Ay! Ya wanna . . . good time?'
She just turned and walked away
And we couldn't believe our luck.

So we drove right up behind her
And made the tyres squeal.
We know what turns a woman on,
A fast guy at the wheel.
We followed her for seven blocks
And let the engine gun
We could tell she liked us
By the way she tried to run.

We're slow driving, loud talkin'
Petrol-headed Carlton Cowboys.
We only look at life
Through a tinted window screen
We're rootin' and tootin'
Primarily the latter
And callin' out
'There's one now boys!
We don't care where we're goin'
And we don't know where we've been
'Cos the fluffy dice
Don't let you see much in between.

Let me tell you 'bout our car
Well you should hear her roar
She's got sheepskin on the muffler
And shagpile on the floor
Stickers on the window
And a big pulsating . . .
Radio
So we can impress each other
Every place we go.

But a man can't drive alone for good
He needs to find a wife
Someone to sit beside him
In the passenger seat of life
I want a girl just like my car
To be a friend of mine
And when I need to use her
She'll turn over every time

We're fast drinkin', non-thinkin'
Petrol head
Double-yellow lines boys
We'll keep cruisin' round
Until we all have died
With CB antennas
About a half a dozen
We're lookin' like a porcupine, boys
But you will know the difference
If we offer you a ride
'Cos a porcupine always has the
Pricks on the outside
(Yes, a porcupine always has the
Pricks on the outside)

Yes you'll find us in the fast lane
Where the traffic's mergin'
Just four guys in the front seat
And every one a virgin.

Remember when the evening news meant an ordinary man in a plain suit sitting behind a simple desk, reading a straightforward account of the day's events?

Remember when the weather reports meant a lone twerp in a vinyl safari suit, pointing at a map with a stick and trying to get the top off a texta-colour?

WELL FORGET IT!!!

THE LIVE EYE NEWS SERVICE IS HERE

Meet hard-hitting Red Surname. The tallest member of the Live Eye Team; alive. Alert. Wavy haired, his timing is excellent . . .

Meet hard-hitting Karen Amber. You'll find her on the streets; incisive, aware, bitter-sweet, human. She's fairly tall for a woman . . .

Meet hard-hitting Eugene Green. He knows news; informed, authoritative, and very tall . . .

SONIA MCMAHON *Wife of the popular Australian ex-Prime Minister who shocked the world press by wearing a high split dress to a US Presidential function. Australia's then first-lady explained later, 'Naturally, if you have a new dress you think of wearing it to the White House'.*

Red, Amber and Green. The hard-hitting Live Eye Team don't just wait for news to happen; they're on the spot, watching, listening, probing, punching and kicking. To bring you the news as it happens.

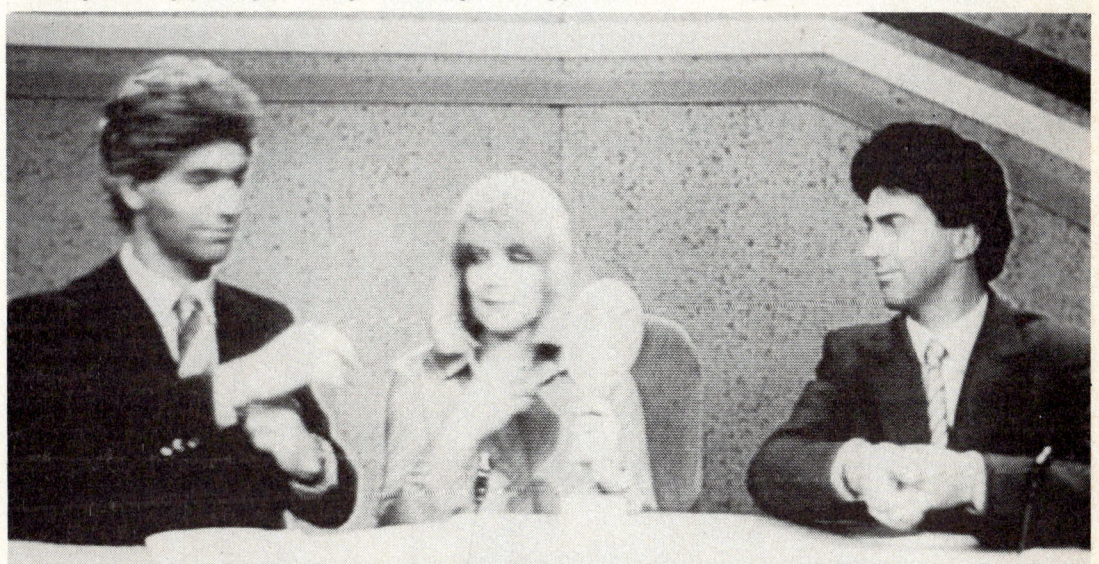

Remember a time before the evening news turned into a fashion parade of intellectual jellyfish, preening themselves in front of the camera, and bringing you regular updates on their personal lives?

NEITHER CAN WE . . .

HOW TO **KILL** YOUR PET

Let's face it. He was a great dog, but you can't be stuffed looking after him any more. OK, what do you do? Well, here is a simple and easy guide to swift death for your four-legged loved one.

1 SCRAPING BRAINS OUT WITH SPOON

2 FLUSHING DOWN THE TOILET (Not recommended for anything larger than a labrador)

3 CHEESE GRATER

4 GASSING (Not recommended for microwaves)

5 DEEP BREATHING

6 DROWNING

You're an Australian.

You know the importance of drinking a light beer, but you still want the full flavour of throwing up in the gutter after closing time.

New 1.1 Extra Light.

Scientifically brewed to allow you to sink over fifty glasses an hour, and still make it home to commit acts of domestic violence on the wife.

Now, can you feel a 1.1 comin' up?

In some countries they don't have advertising . . .

No, in some countries they don't have an endless stream of drivel about the latest load of useless overseas rubbish being dumped on local markets at enormous profit. In some countries they don't have advertising.
IF YOU'D LIKE TO VISIT THESE COUNTRIES, PHONE *KAY'S TRAVEL*

THE JOY OF AUSSIE SEX
'The Sheep Dip'

POSITION 7:

(National Party Voter on top, Merino Ewe on bottom.)

SIR JOH BJELKE-PETERSEN Peanut, grazier and democratically elected Premier of Queensland since 1968, Sir Joh is best known for his tireless efforts in the areas of Aboriginal land rights, civil liberties and environmental issues. He has fought them all.

A BICENTENNIAL HYMN

Australians all let us rejoice
For we have come this far
Let's share a beer for two hundred years
And throw up in the car.
Our land abounds in nature's gifts
Across the rich red sands
From birds caged up to dam-drowned pups
And roos in pet food cans.
These centuries two we've made it through
On a winged keel and a prayer
In virulent strain then let us sing
Advance Australia, Where?

THE BIG ONE

*Winning entry in the Bicentenary 'Write the New
National Anthem' Competition.*

You know, there's a man they call 'the ringer'
When he's bringin' in the sheep.
His hands are broad, his back is bent,
His eyes are blue and deep.

He's a true blue Aussie worker.
You ask him and he'll say,
'When I work for Australia
It gets bigger every day.'

(chorus) Australia's got a big one,
The biggest in the land.
Yes, we've got a big one,
Hey, come on, lend a hand!
To make our big one bigger,
Inch by inch as it's unfurled.
By rule of thumb we figure
It's the biggest in the world.

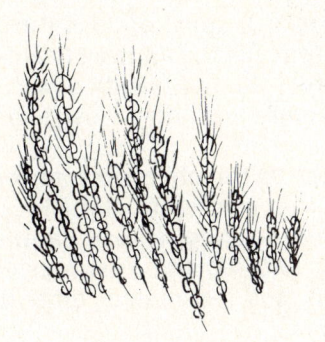

Our wheat, our sheep, our shopping-jeeps,
Far as the eye can see.
The big Australian emptiness –
It's big enough for me!

But there are some who say we're nothing;
That we haven't got the strength.
Let's show them we can reach the top –
Let's give the world a length!

(chorus)

Australia's got a big one,
Each man, each boy, each girl.
A whopper of a big one.
It's the biggest in the world
Australia's got a big one,
Each man, each boy, each girl.
A whopper of a big one.
It's the biggest in the world.

TRAVELOGUE
Welcome to Australia!
So you finally made it!

For those of you who've never had the Down Under Experience before,
be prepared for the holiday of a lifetime!
Enjoy the exciting nightlife of our clean, modern cities!
Experience the excitement! and rugged beauty of the Outback!
Or just lie back and soak up the sun on a palm-fringed beach in tropical, island Paradise.

With so many of the world's most spectacular natural and man-made wonders all in the one place, Australia's got something for everyone!

So if it's excitement! adventure! or just plain old relaxation you're after – Australia's the place for you!

But be warned – you may never want to leave!

Australia is a land of great contrasts so make sure you experience as much of it as you can!

THE ALPS – PLAYGROUND OF AUSTRALIA

Although not as big as the European Alps there is still lots of fun to be had 'weekending' in the Australian Snowfields.

Be sure to rug up, though! Australian alpine regions are just as cold as European ones, and several large parties of Swiss ski-enthusiasts have perished horribly as a direct result of their smug complacency.

THE DESERT

Those of you with a spirit of adventure! may not be able to resist the alluring beauty of the Red Centre – the hot, sandy deserts and silent serenity of the Australian Outback.

If you *do* choose to travel between major cities make sure that you report at the local post-office before leaving (most capital cities have one) and tell the Post Master your destination and estimated time of arrival.

Remember that distances in Australia are much greater than anywhere else in the world; so try to think in terms of weeks, months or years rather than the inconceivable number of kilometres or miles. This will help you to get a much better grasp of the situation and so maintain a positive outlook/remain calm/avoid panic.

Most Post Masters will be more than happy to supply you with a packet of butter and thermometer: remember! A nasty sunburn could ruin your fun!

So take plenty of water, a terry-towelling hat, DO NOT DRINK YOUR OWN URINE and take off on the adventure! holiday of a lifetime!

Australia

A NATURALIST'S PARADISE!

Here's just a few of the beautiful and exotic creatures *you* might come across on a holiday adventure downunder . . .

Blue-Ringed Octopus (WA)

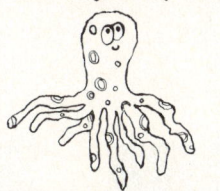

Sting causes death due to respiratory failure which is instant and excruciating. If victim does survive, s/he will vomit, have trouble breathing, experience speech difficulties and lapse into unconsciousness. Convalescence may take weeks. However, bookings for any of Western Australia's coastal resorts must be made months in advance.

Box Jelly Fish (Qld)

The sting of the Box Jelly Fish causes an indescribable pain and frenzied convulsions that lead to agonising death within three minutes. Found in Queensland's tropical north, the area is a must for beach lovers.

Funnel Web Spider (NSW)

The fangs of the Funnel Web can penetrate light clothing, causing immediate and indescribable pain throughout the body, sweaty delirium and eventually respiratory failure, leading to death within ninety seconds. Breath-taking harbour views make sunny Sydney an absolute *must* on every travel itinerary.

Great White Shark (Vic)

Shark bites usually cause an extensive, ragged, messy wound which may contain fragments of bone, damaged tissue and shark teeth, as well as a penicillin resistant bacteria. Never urinate, defecate or dangle limbs over the edge of a boat when passing through southern Victoria.

Scrub Tick (SA)

NEVER pull the bloated body of a blood-sucking Scrub Tick from the victim's flesh, as the head will remain embedded and spread its toxic salivary excretions, causing local anaesthesia, then more generalised toxaemia and paralysis. Similar results may be produced by a tour of the Barossa Valley.

Dingo (NT)

Completely harmless. Possibly the gentlest creature God ever put breath into.

AUSTRALIA! AN UNFORGETTABLE HOLIDAY EXPERIENCE!!!

MRS MARY CULLEN Pioneer Catholic reformer. In 1964 Mary sought to have all bikinis banned from Australian beaches for fear they would 'lower the resistance of young people to temptation and contribute to immorality'.

Love Is Love

Signora Santospirito
My daughter, my baby, how could she do it?

Mrs Glickenstein
My son, mein only boy. We did everything for him, and now he wants to ruin it all by marrying a Catholic.

Signora Santospirito
We did everything for her: locked her in a convent, and let her go to dances once a year, with her brother.

Mrs Glickenstein
What will Rabbi Levine say? He circumcised my boy; made his bar mitzvah, and even arranged the finance on his first block of flats.

Signora Santospirito
Father Pietro has known her since she was a baby. He baptised her, gave her first holy communion, absolved her after her first abor. . . er, miscarriage (I always said that it was an accident.)

Mrs Glickenstein
What was wrong with Naomi Finkelstein? She was a good girl, good family, good figure – the nose could be fixed.

Signora Santospirito
What was wrong with Giuseppe next door? He loved her, said he would marry her – despite the moustache.

Mrs Glickenstein
Maybe she trapped my boy. Tells him she's pregnant, but still a virgin, so he'll marry her. Wouldn't be the first Jewish boy to fall for that one.

Signora Santospirito
My daughter, she couldn't be pregnant – again. I talk to her, I tell her all the modern ways for a girl to take precautions. Standing on her hand, lighting a candle to the patron saint of falling downstairs.

Mrs Glickenstein
Too busy crossing herself, should have crossed her legs.

Signora Santospirito
What about the ceremony? We have different beliefs, different gods.

Mrs Glickenstein
Who will do the catering?

MARRIAGE CELEBRANT'S GUIDEBOOK
The Mudbrick Wedding

Friends, (insert names of both parties) have called us here today to witness and share in their marriage, as they become person and person.

They bring to this marriage the experiences, joys, and friendships which they have accumulated through their (insert number) previous marriages, de facto relationships (do not count one-night stands or even more casual sexual encounters).

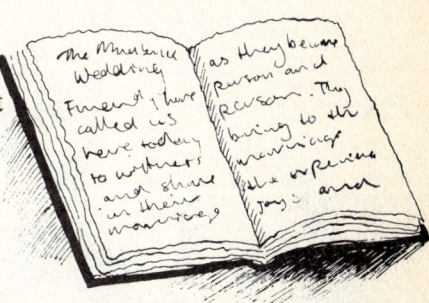

To Female
Do you, (insert name), take (insert name), to be your lawfully wedded person? And do you agree on every second weekend to take care of Kylie, Jason and Jim from his first marriage to Shiela (insert star sign); Tristan, Liam, and Kelly from his second marriage to Shiela (insert medicare number) on alternate Wednesdays; in addition to raising as your own, his love-children, Bliss, Earth-flute and Zevon from his union with that crazy gypsy lady who left him two years ago to study astrology with The Master, Morning Star (insert distance from sun in light-years.

To Male
And do you, (insert name), take (insert name), in a very caring and completely non-sexist way to be your lawfully wedded person? And do you respect her right, as an individual, to go on seeing Manning (insert hair colour), the bass guitarist, whom she still cares for but is kind of confused about and whom she still needs to talk to from time to time; along with Tagbosh O'Reilly (insert huge laugh), whom she doesn't so much love as feel strongly attracted to in a weird kind of basic physical way?

To Both
Would you please exchange all previous marriage deeds, land titles, divorce settlement papers, and children?

In the presence of these witnesses, I now pronounce you person and person.

You may now commence group massage.

THE JOY OF AUSSIE SEX
'The Missionary Position'

POSITION 53:

(Christian zealot on bottom, bondage mistress on top.)

HAROLD HOLT *The popular PM who went 'all the way with LBJ', trebling Australia's war commitment in Vietnam and, in March 1966, sending young military conscripts into battle.*

Boys Own Adventure!!!

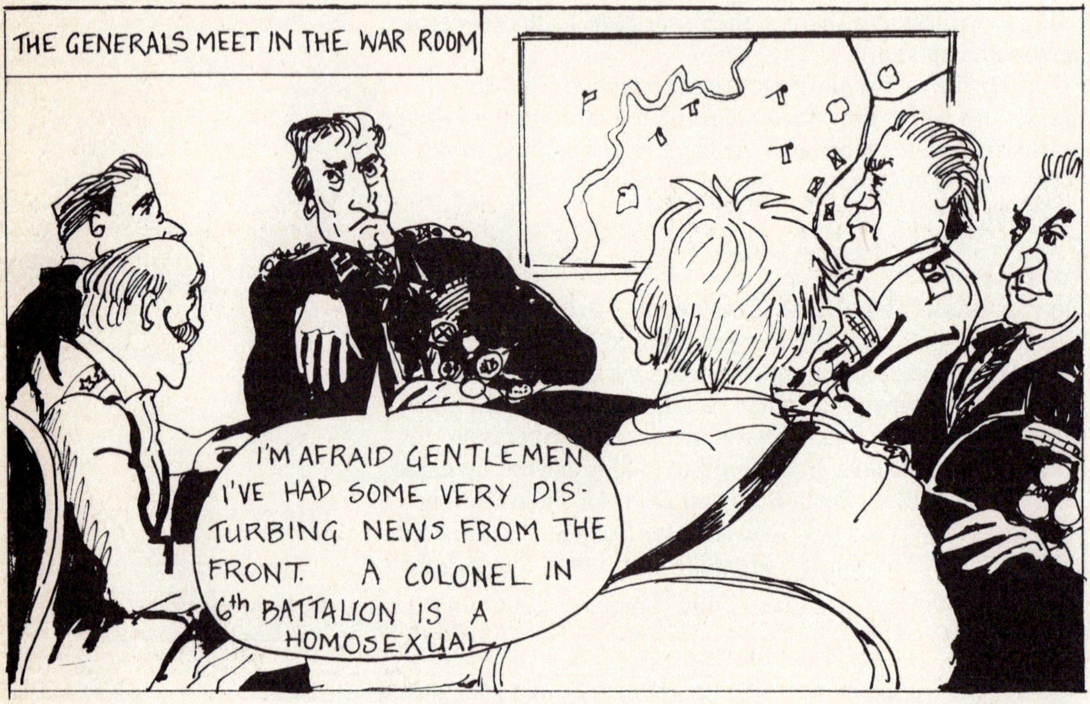

THE GENERALS MEET IN THE WAR ROOM

I'M AFRAID GENTLEMEN I'VE HAD SOME VERY DISTURBING NEWS FROM THE FRONT. A COLONEL IN 6th BATTALION IS A HOMOSEXUAL

A CRISIS IS LOOMING AT HQ

MAJOR CARTER HERE TELLS ME THAT YOU'RE A HOMOSEXUAL. IS THAT TRUE?!

I SAW HIM SIR - WITH HIS PANTS DOWN

IT IS SIR. I FELL IN LOVE WITH THE GERMAN POW

NEWS SPREADS FAST THROUGH THE FRONT......

DIER COLONEL IS A POOF

I'LL PASS IT ON

DID YOU HEAR THAT! THE COLONEL IS A POOF

72

73

Continued page 134 . . .

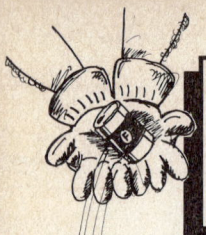

RODNEY MARSH *A legendary Australian wicket-keeper, Marsh holds the record for catches taken in Test cricket and cans of beer consumed on a flight between Australia and England (48). Upon landing at Heathrow the champion athlete had to be wheeled off the plane in a luggage trolley by fellow Test cricketing hero, D.K. Lillee.*

OUR FABULOUS SPORTING DECADE
Great moments in the last 10 years of Aussie Sporting Triumphs

1976 | Montreal Olympics. Australia scores one bronze medal.

1977 | Queensland's first dwarf throwing competition.

1978 | Australian surfers forced to undergo Peroxide tests.

1979 | Two spectators at the Melbourne Cup accidentally see the race.

1980 | Mean Machine swimming team disqualified after urine tests (of the pool).

1981 | Dennis Lillee kicks Pakistani captain for being short, black and a great batsman.

1982 | Spectator killed by flying beer can at Princes Park (Vic)

1983 | Four Queensland racehorses found dead.
Lisa Curry and Grant Kenny marry and produce high fibre commercials.

1984 | Test fast bowler Geoff Lawson is awarded the highest accolade available to modern cricketers – the offer of a second McDonald's commercial.

1985 | Geoffrey Edlesten opens VFL jumble sale.

1986 | The Victorian town of Moyston hosts the 20th annual Rabbit Skinning Competition. Previous year's winner, Ron 'Killer' Crawford, battles sciatic nerve problems to take out the title.

> **KIM HUGHES** Top aussie test hero who, in 1985, was driven to tears before flying to South Africa for a national tour.

Reaction from the fans

Dear Sir,

As a long time opponent of racism, I believe the system of apartheid in South Africa must be abolished. That's why myself and eleven other Australian cricketers felt the need to tour this country – purely as a gesture of protest. Only by seeing the problems of racial injustice first hand can we ever hope to address them. And what better way to do this than by playing a full test series with additional one day matches in particular troublespots. We hope that other Australian sportsmen and women will follow our lead and organise sporting protest tours for themselves, so that they too can learn of the crippling injustice that is apartheid. The lads and I are determined to return next summer, just to take another squizz at the appalling situation that is South Africa – and maybe boost our batting averages. In fact, most of us are banking on it.

Yours tearfully

(Written on behalf of a number of people)

Dear Editor,

I was shocked to read that 'Knackers' Barnburg, one of this country's most gifted and ruthlessly brutal sportsmen, had been given two weeks suspension for throat slashing in the final quarter of last Saturday's home and away match. I ask you; if they take the violence out of professional football, what will we be left with? A pack of Nancy Boys running around after a flaming bit of leather! In the old days, you'd run out on to the ground and, for two hours, try to smash as many peoples' heads in as possible. Then you'd run off again. They were great days; days when you could tell the worth of a bloke by the way he physically abused you. Many of your younger readers may not remember 'Scragger' Murray, one of the best centre half-backs in the league. Now, to be honest, when I first met 'Scragger', I thought he was a fairy. Within two minutes, I was in a coma. He was a great sportsman, as was old 'Biffer' O'Brien. I remember setting on old 'Biffer' with a chainsaw in the '38 Grand Final and removing a couple of his more 'vital' organs. And you know what he said to me in the hospital afterwards? That he respected me? No! That he worshiped me. That's the sort of bloke he was, God rest him. Let me conclude by saying that I don't respect anyone, man, woman or child, unless I've first beaten them senseless.

Yours sincerely

Percival 'Cracker' McGuire

(Northland Home for the Criminally Aged)

The Sunday

WIN UNLIMITED SEX WITH A TOT
What a fabulous contest

*** Look at all these exclamation marks
!!!!!!!!!!!!!!!!!!!!!!!!!!!!!!!**

POPE MASTURBATES IN FRONT OF CROWD!

QUEEN'S GAY LOVE-CHILD NAKED *AIDS* SEX ROMP!

Trevor Pope, 63, of East Bentleigh, was charged and convicted for indecent exposure in front of two members of the Croydon Women's Bowling Club.

Joh has Aids!!

Affable Premier of QLD, Joh Bjelke Peterson has bought a set of hearing aids.

Reagan's Huge Prick

President of USA Ronald Reagan is reported to have a very large penis.

IN THIS WEEK'S DAILY CRAP

* AIDS Victim Wheelchair Agony P3
* Boy George Speaks Out on AIDS Addiction P7
* Abbreviators Shot 'n Stabbed in Slap 'n Tickle Romp. Lots 'o Blood
* More Bullshit About Actors who have AIDS
* 'I don't have AIDS' – Robert De Castella
* Sport: Greyhounds Chase AIDS Rabbit

Her Royal Highness, Q. Elizabeth II.

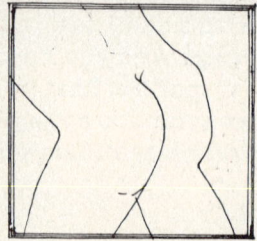

A bum.

FULL STORY P.2.

DEATHS

ARKWRIGHT, Ted
(Suddenly) Loved husband of Noelene (dec.), loving father of Susan (dec.), David (dec.), James (dec.), and grand-pop of Matthew (dec.). Sadly missed by absolutely no one.

CULLEN, Bernie
(Drunkenly) After twenty-eight pots and a cream sherry, fell backwards and cracked his head on the cigarette machine. Fondest memories from all his mates at The Bridge. Rest in piss.

WOLLSTON, George
(Finally) Irritable and incontinent father of Steve, father-in-law of Megan, after a regrettably short illness. You were a tiresome old man who wouldn't stop going on and on about 'the good old days' and your bloody war mates who'll probably all show up after the funeral expecting another feed – no wonder the Repat. agreed to turn off your drip. At last Megan and I can fumigate the bungalow and melt down those bloody old war medals to help pay for Tiffany's braces. Rest in peace, Dad.

ZWEILLER, Jan
To my loving wife: 'I can't believe you're no longer mine And this ad costs five bucks a line.'

CLASSIFIEDS

PHILLIPS
The funeral service of Mrs J Phillips will be held at the Claystown Crematorium at 11.00 this Friday, total fire bans permitting. In lieu of flowers, please send cash cheques to Arthur Brimscotti and Sons. We specialise in all funeral services.

This week's special: Cremations $850 ($900 and you keep the ashes).

Plus a complete range of surplus coffins – see our van out the back of the general cemetery every Friday night.

BIRTHS

PRESCOTT, Geoff and Heather
A girl. Thanks to all staff and doctors at the Sydney Acupuncture Centre for a painless delivery. Mother and porcupine both doing well.

RYAN, Pat and Eileen
We are pleased to announce the arrival of our ninth child. Thanks to all staff at the Catholic Family Planning Centre for another joyous blessing from God. Baby doing well. Mother dead.

WILSON, Myra and Des
A love child by natural (underwater) birth. Thanks to manager and staff at the City Baths for clearing the pool so quickly. Sorry about the afterbirth.

STILL BIRTHS

SINCLAIR, Patrice
Last Thursday, tripped coming down the stairs.

JINDAWARRA, Jacki Jacki
At the Maralinga Public Hospital. Grateful thanks to the British Army.

ENGAGEMENTS

CREIGHTON, Dimitrioulos
Rev. & Mrs G. Creighton of Adelaide are pleased to announce the engagement of their only daughter Stephanie to the greasy looking son of our greengrocer.

SITS VAC

WANTED
Migrant ladies with little or no understanding of minimum wage regulations to earn virtually nothing by sewing for a prominent fashion designer.

Earn Big Money in your own home!!!
Become an SP Bookmaker. Contact Sgt. Cranston, NSW CIB today.

Having a Kids Party?
Pete the Magic Clown is now out on probation, and ready to handle your child's next big occasion.

"UNCLE STAN'S LULLABY"

(To tune of "3 Blind Mice")

Pae-do-phile. Pae-do-phile. See how he runs!

See how he runs! He waits for little boys all on their own.

Outside the shelter shed, follow them home. Have you ever

been caught in a safety zone? With a pae-do-phile!

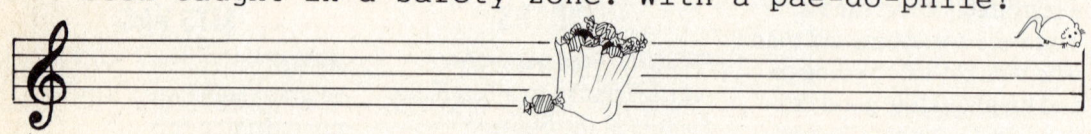

(The children form a circle, holding hands and skipping around until the word "zone" – then they all fall over and come down to my place for iced vo-vos).

Can you spot the difference in these 2 pictures? (Hint: there are at least 3!)

There are at least 3 animals hidden in this Northern Territory campfire scene. See if you can spot them!

What's Skip got hidden in his bag of iced chocs? Join the dots to find out!

BRUCE RUXTON Popular Victorian President of the RSL since 1979. Bruce has long since buried the hatchet with our Japanese aggressors. He has, however, suggested that Vietnamese refugees arriving on our shores should be towed back out to sea and sunk.

The full excitement of the America's Cup Defence won't be upon us until 1987

Yet already, many of Australia's northern neighbors are setting sail for Alan Bond's Sun City,

eager to put these lovingly crafted vessels through their paces in the all-important twelve-metre challenge.

Soon, the manly sweat of competition will wash the salt of the Timor Sea from their tear-ducts,

while the West Australian sun bleaches their hair to spun-gold.

And on that special day when new Australians join true Australians in the vital pursuit of yachting excellence, they may yet taste from the Great Silver Cup

a new beer so light – so refreshing – it just has to be the drink for today.

The America's Cup, a host of thirsty refugees and Swan Special Light.

A WINNING COMBINATION.

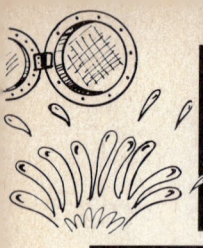

FROM THE 'TWELVE INCH STUD'

I often read your Forum section and, like many other people, I always thought it was just made up – that is, until something very incredible happened to me last summer.

It was a hot day, and as my wife was away for the weekend, I was driving along the coast by myself with nothing much to do. Then up ahead, I noticed a couple of female hitch-hikers. I never pick up strangers on the road, but I thought to myself, 'Hell, I haven't got much to do anyway.' I pulled over and they got in.

What happened after that will always remain etched in my memory. Cindy, the blonde, sat in the passenger's seat next to me, and within a few minutes asked whether I minded if she knitted. Not believing my luck, I said, 'sure'. Meanwhile, in the rear-vision mirror, I noticed Candy, the other blonde, stretched out all the way in the back seat, obviously having a nap.

My palms began to sweat as Cindy, the first blonde, reached over and pointed outside, saying, 'Aren't those eucalypts fascinating?' My wife never said those kinds of things to me, and already I was beginning to think of the long night ahead.

Before I knew it, the two girls, both blonde, asked if we could stop for a drink of water in the next town. I

could hardly conceal my excitement. We drove for a little while longer, and my eyes almost dropped out of my head when I turned around to see Candy, one of the blondes, fully clothed while reading a book! Until then, I thought these things only happened in films.

Soon we came to a small town. Without wasting a moment of time, we rushed to the nearest rest-rooms. Again, I could hardly believe my luck – we were the only ones there. By this time, Cindy, the blonde, couldn't control herself any more – she was dying for a drink. She bent over the tap, giving me a perfect view of her luscious duffle-coat. Cindy, the non-brunette, joined in straight away, and in no time, was drying her hands with a paper towel. I thought I'd get in on the action, so I got in between them and started combing my hair.

Wow. I never thought it could be like this, but today all my dreams were coming true. Candy just couldn't stop drinking the water, she was so thirsty. As for Cindy, by now she was tying up her shoelace. As you might expect, I wasted no time in tucking my shirt in.

'Let's eat', said Candy. What a woman! I thought she'd had enough excitement for one day, but this chick was insatiable.

We spent the rest of the day eating potato cakes, driving through interesting country-side, singing Boney M songs, playing Trivial Pursuit and, as a final climax, we

discussed in depth the devaluation of the Australian dollar.

When I dropped them off, I thanked them for the trip of a lifetime, for the pleasure and the rewards. They thanked me for the ride and said the pleasure was all theirs. As they walked away, I realised I would never see them again.

– *(name witheld by request)*

'ABSOLUTE CRAP'

I'd like to share an experience that happened to me last week. I was at the supermarket, and had sex with twelve checkout girls, fifteen frustrated housewives, seven lesbians, and seventy-four negresses. Every single one of them had over two hundred orgasms each, and I found the G-Spots of over 99.97 per cent of them. They all said I was an absolutely fantastic lover (I guess I *am* pretty well-hung) and they all wanted to pay me lots of money for satisfying them.

(name witheld)

PS A good friend of mine would like to know where he could meet girls.

PPS Could you send a copy of your reply to me? Another friend of mine needs the information.

C E N T R E F O L D

Name: Sr Mary Therese

Bust: 36 **WAIST:** 26 **HIPS** 36

Height: 5'7" **WEIGHT:** 117 **SIGN:** Carmellite

Birth Date: 11/2/58 **BIRTH PLACE:** Adelaide, Australia

Goals: To continue spiritual life as a novitiate within the convent and complete my vows; or become an actress.

Turn-ons: Retreats, Papal bulls, Bishop Desmond Tutu, Silent prayer, the touch of a silk wimple.

Turn-offs: Stale communion wafers, long sermons, anything C of E

Favourite Foods: Angel Cake

Favourite Musicians: Sr Janet Mead, Mary O'Hara, early Van Halen

Favourite Books: Summa Theologiae, any of the Gospels, *Hollywood Wives.*

Favourite Pastime: I love to do total body massage. Starting at the feet, working each bone in the foot, then legs, not missing an inch of your body, all the way up to the eyes. I also collect holy cards.

WANTED: SURROGATE MOTHER

No experience required! Earn big money!

Healthy child = $10,000
More than 2 weeks prem. = $5,000
Miscarriage = $200 (and you get to keep the afterbirth)
Guaranteed – CASH ON DELIVERY!!!
PO BOX 142
QLD

THE JOY OF AUSSIE SEX
The Standard Position
POSITION 73:

(Lights out, man on top, finish within 2 minutes.)

A COMPLETE GUIDE TO SEX EDUCATION FOR AUSTRALIAN BOYS & GIRLS

A Time Of Change!

Between the ages of ten and sixteen most people notice various changes taking place in their bodies. For example, menstruation begins, new body hair appears and the breasts grow markedly in size.

Girls experience similar developments. This is all perfectly normal and absolutely nothing to be ashamed of. Yet. It is all part of God's long term plan for us to become parents and bring children of our own into the world.

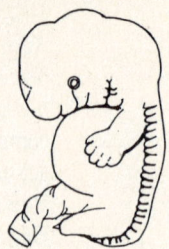

EIGHT WEEKS

How Life Begins

With the exception of some very simple forms of life that reproduce by non-sexual means (e.g. starfish, dung beatles, nuns), all species rely on the process of fertilisation. This occurs when a man (husband) and a woman (wife) turn out the lights (i.e. foreplay) and lie together for anything up to thirty seconds. The man then falls asleep and a new life begins.

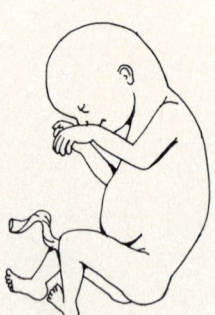

THREE MONTHS

The Sexual Organs

By now, you'll probably have noticed that men (husbands) and women (wives) are built differently from each other. Men have a penis and testes. Women don't.

When the man (husband) becomes aroused, his penis stiffens or becomes erect. It is then that a very special thing takes place – he comes home from the pub and commences the act of fertilisation.

MALE SEXUAL ORGANS (ACTUAL SIZE)

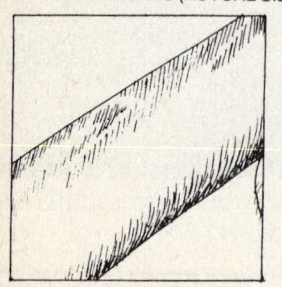

FEMALE SEXUAL ORGANS

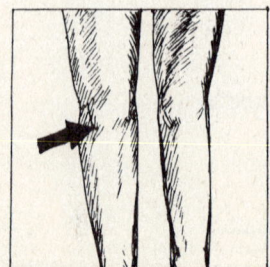

SEVEN YEARS

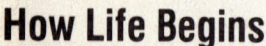

Birth Control

ABSTINENCE

Sometimes a man and a woman may decide they don't want to share in the joys of childbirth. These selfish couples are usually motivated by health considerations, marital difficulties, or the fact that Section 6, paragraph (e) of the *Income Tax Assessment Act* imposes a marginal rate of 48 per cent on a child's earnings, negating the whole point of income splitting arrangements. To prevent unwanted pregnancy, a man and a woman must practise birth control, or *contraception* (contra from the Greek word to go against, 'ception' from the Latin 'BBQ or wedding reception' hence, to go against the BBQ) There are several techniques of birth control.

 THE PILL

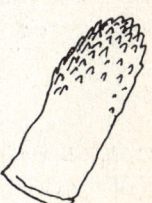

CONDOM (RIBBED)

SOME FREQUENTLY ASKED QUESTIONS

Q Does masturbation cause insanity or pimples?
A No, this is an old wives' tale. Masturbation causes blindness.

Q Is penis size important to women?
A Yes, very.

SPERMICIDE SPRAY

Q What is PMT?
A PMT stands for pre-menstrual tension, a recurrent affliction suffered by women which prevents them from holding jobs of any great responsibility. PMT has been linked with nervous tension, violent tendencies and the fall of the Australian dollar.

Q Do women have sexual urges like men?
A No. Any woman who notices strange desires should immediately consult the family doctor or a *gynaecologist* (a gynaecologist is a doctor who specialises in the short-term money market).

COITUS INTERRUPTUS

Q What is VD?
A The natural product of teenage promiscuity and end-of-season football trips. The word venereal is derived from the word Venus, the Roman Goddess of Penicillin.

Q Is necking or heavy petting dangerous?
A Not in itself; however, as a general rule, anything that is not done with parental supervison is fraught with problems.

A Glossary of Australian Words and Phrases

ASIO
Australian Security and Intelligence Organisation (spot the contradiction in terms).

BILLABONG
Small backwater (see Adelaide).

THE BLUE HEELER
Bred specifically for droving and rounding up sheep, the blue heeler is a *silent* and *tireless* worker.

However, in *lean times* when work opportunities *are scarce*, the heeler may experience severe forms of *despair* and *melancholia,* arising from a *crisis of meaning* in the dog's life.

Common signs to look out for are a pervasive *listlessness* and a *disinclination* to be drawn into group activities. The dog will be noticeably less *cheery.* He may also speak of a certain sense of *emotional* and *spiritual desolation* and care should be taken that the dog is not allowed to become too *introspective.*

Do not attempt to jolly him out of his mood.
This will only depress him further.

BULL-BAR
Device affixed to the front of a vehicle to prevent damage when driving through Australian fauna.

BUNYIP
Known by Aboriginals as Devil Devil, this mythical creature is so feared that they will not cross a stream or river if it is thought to be inhabited by one (also known as sewerage outlet).

DIGGERS
Aussie soldiers generally considered to be taller, broader, stronger and more blonde than any other foreign force, who died in our nation's two great wars. (c.f. Vietnam Vets, who are short and quite dark-haired).

FOOTBALL
Or 'Footy' is a game of great pace and excitement in which teams of eighteen men and twenty-three accountants try to drive the ball back and forth along an oval, whilst staying financially solvent. The long kicks, high catches (marks) and sudden take-over bids make footy a truly great contact sport.

FLUFFY DICE
A secular St Christopher medal carried in automobiles.

MOCCASINS
(Not in polite usage) Footwear intended for use indoors.

MOLE
A woman who blindly and irrationally persists in her refusal to let a bloke sleep with her just because he's had a few drinks.

MULESING
The quaint practice of tearing skin from around a sheep's anus without the aid of anaesthetic.

SWAGMAN (as in 'once a jolly')
Itinerant labourer not covered by Federal or State award wages.

POOFTA
(Not indigenous) A male who displays an unnatural interest in the arts or light beer.

ROOT
(As in wanna —) would you like the fibrous underground stock of a plant; or to have sex with an Australian male, whichever seems the more appealing.

Also, vital in providing a very funny joke about a wombat.

SACRED SITE See Uranium Mine.

SCRUBBER
Woman (other than mother or sister) who engages in sexual activity prior to marriage.

URANIUM MINE See Sacred Site.

HOROSCOPE

HOROSCOPE by Santo the Magnificent

GEMINI All of you will die tomorrow. There will be no escape.

AQUARIUS Beware of square objects, especially those with triangles at the bottom.[1]

PISCES Beware of falling off tall buildings.[2]

LEO I don't know.[3]

SAGITTARIUS See Capricorn.

SCORPIO Do not drink and drive as penalties can be very stiff.[4]

TAURUS During an electrical storm, one can see the electrical discharge of the clouds in the distance.[5]

ARIES Your period could come earlier than expected.

LIBRA An expedition to Tierra del Fuego should not be undertaken this month.[6]

CAPRICORN See Sagittarius.

CANCER Many problems will arise this month; friends will make demands, you may meet a dark stranger, watch your finances, go to a disco and have sex with someone.[7]

VIRGO You will die one day. (So will everyone else.)

FOOTNOTES

1 A herd of sheep does not qualify.

2 A house is not a tall building, it is generally considered that anything above ten stories is tall. Twenty stories is very tall.

3 Sorry.

4 Loss of liscence above 0.15

5 This belongs on page forty-three.

6 If you must go, tell someone where you are going.

7 Sex is good.

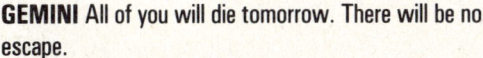

Dealer East
All vulnerable

```
                    NORTH
                    ♠ KQ52
                    ♥ AKJ104
                    ♦ 42
                    ♣ A4
        WEST                    EAST
        ♠ J106                  ♠ A
        ♥ Q7                    ♥ 9863
        ♦ J108753              ♦ A96
        ♣ J6                   ♣ KQ983
                    SOUTH
                    ♠ 98743
                    ♥ 52
                    ♦ KQ
                    ♣ 10752
```

East	South	West	North
2C(1)	Pass	Pass	X
Pass	2S	Pass	3C
Pass	3S	Pass	4S
All pass			

South was declarer in four spades against the lead of the club jack, with only three losers in an attempt to bring the contract home with a diamond at trick two, while cashing the club king on a four-card major and East's excited diamond to declarer's king. Declarer must lose trump trick to East's 5clubs, with 9diamonds on East West, he need not have spade ace for opening bid. South must stay clear of East's club king and West's cigar smoke and North's garlic breath.

East doesn't attempt trump promotion by third round clubs at trick four, offering attractive defence, against West's spade ace and declarer promotion second trump third round heart ruff, spade position on ace bare, dummy spade 2!!!! Accordingly, low spade at trick 5 to declarer bidding, North's nose picking, halitosis, right wing arrogant hearts queen second trump trick bringing a well scored +630.

A fine performance.

This page is blank

ALSO AVAILABLE IN PENGUIN BOOKS . . .

THE COMPLETE WORKS OF SHAKESPEARE

All the immortal plays from the noble barn in one easy-to-store volume. Includes *Macbeth*, *As You Like It* and the unforgettable *South Pacific*.

HELMINTHS, ARTHROPODS AND PROTOZOA OF PRIMARY INVERTEBRATES

A *must* for every camera enthusiast!

LICENSED TO KILL
Alistair Porter

Garry Beckwell is a wanted man. Chased to South America by MI5 and the CIA, he meets Leena – a Mexican peasant girl who falls instantly in love with his handsomely-chiselled features. Then gets killed. Another action-packed thriller from Australia's master of suspense.

VETS MIGHT MAKE MONEY
J Herriot

The delightful sequel to *All Bank Statements Great and Small*, *Vet in Money* and *Let Wealthy Vets Lie*

LICENSED TO KILL AGAIN
Alistair Porter

Grant Stedwell is a spy. Wanted by several international organisations in Europe, he meets Ingrid – a Swedish peasant girl who falls madly in love with him. And gets killed. Another gripping saga from Australia's master of the spy novel.

THIS IS SUNBURNT AUSTRALIA

The ultimate coffee table book! Think how great this will look propped up against those back copies of *Belle* magazine. Over 200 full-colour photographs and a guaranteed maximum of only ten words (in large type) on any given page. The book with skin cancer . . .

FLOWERS
Alistair Porter

Garth Tredwell is gay and shares a flat with several friends in Balmain. A change of direction from Australia's greatest spy novelist.

ONE HUNDRED NOT OUT
Sir Keith Stumper, OBE

A delightful collection of cricketing anecdotes from one of Australia's oldest farts. Read how Keith feels the modern game is being destroyed by poor sportsmanship, white balls and rubber-soled playing shoes. If only we had another good war – knock some sense into those colour-uniformed pansies. I remember the tied test of '58 . . . etc.

DAS KAPITAL
Geoff Marx

The complete guide to Canberra's natural beauty. Includes full colour photographs by Barbara Engels.

THE MYSTERY OF WOODLEIGH MANOR
Agatha Smith

Smith spins a classic tale of murder, incest and suspense which will keep the reader breathless from page one to the final, shock denoument in which the killer is unmasked. (It was the dental nurse.)

THE KING JAMES POP-UP BIBLE
God

As used by nine out of ten Protestant clerics. Aaron's rod has never looked this good!

WHEN LOVE KNOCKS TWICE
Barbara Hartland

Pretty Polly Anglosaxonsurname had only just moved to the small English village of Tuxbridge when she met Tom, a handsome doctor/merchant banker/lawyer (insert dominant male profession of your own choice . . .)

MORE ABOUT PENGUINS: if you've enjoyed this book and would like to know more about the other works mentioned above, just send 30p (if you live in England) or $6½ million (if you live in Australia) and we'll refer you to the appropriate psychiatric institution.

NB This book is sold by weight not volume. Some settling of contents may have occurred during shipment and handling.

MARIO MILANO *Champion Australian wrestler, Mario was our first bi-linguist to fully master the abdominal stretch.*

TO: The International Olympic Committee, Geneva.
FROM: Reg Burrows, Shire President, Dubbo.
RE: Application to host 22nd Olympic Games, 1988

The warmth and hospitality that is Dubbo is legendary throughout North-Eastern NSW. Known as 'The Gateway to Semi-arid Grazing Land', Dubbo attracts 100s of tourists every year with its exciting array of hotels, clubs and non-banking financial institutions; and, of course, our annual Hydrangea Festival. But, even as I write, extra-special preparations are underway to prepare Dubbo as the host city of the 1988 Olympic Games!

Facilities The sporting facilities here in Dubbo are second to none. Our Olympic-size pool is running at least six months of every year, and Mrs Culthorn has agreed to let the marathon go through her bottom paddock as long as all gates are shut (and she can meet that nice young man with the black moustache).

Accommodation We have a list of possible billets, and the Ladies' Association is cooking jam, and preparing lamingtons. However, it would be appreciated if each athlete competing could bring a plate.

Crowd Control Dubbo extends the rectal glove of friendship to all competitors and spectators. Chief Constable Murnane feels more than confident about coping with the expected influx of 500,000 visitors, as both police cars are now fully operational. One request however; we'd prefer no blacks as in our experience they tend to drink a bit – I think you know what we mean. (Asiatics are most welcome, and the RSL are prepared to bury the hatchet).

Proposed Exhibition Sports Dwarf throwing, Cane toad kicking (very popular up north), wet T-shirt competitions (very popular nationally).

Well, there you have it. All we need now is the I.O.C.'s go-ahead. The council certainly doesn't wish to influence your decision (hope you enjoyed the Premiership Port), but remember, our municipal incinerator stands ready for that Olympic Flame to burn (depending on total fire bans).
Yours sincerely,

(Reg Burrows).

P.S. We would appreciate a prompt reply as we have to start organising the Hydrangea Festival.

AMERICA'S CUP

INTERVIEWER Preparations are under way for the defence of the America's Cup. We spoke to Alan about the organisation behind keeping the Cup in Australian hands.

ALAN It's going very well, we're pretty much ahead of schedule at this stage, the theme song's been recorded, it's a catchy little tune, a bit loud, but I'm sure the young ones will like it. The Prime Minister's coat has been finished, it's a bit loud, but he'll like it. The victory parade has been organised, fireworks — that sort thing — and we've sold the TV rights to a very innovative American network for live prime time broadcast.

INTERVIEWER American prime time?

ALAN Yes, we'll be staging the race in the middle of the night.

INTERVIEWER Who exactly will be competing?

ALAN The Yanks of course, English, Italians. French team looks strong — they're not sending a yacht, just a couple of divers. The Kiwis are sending a boat — but we might appeal against them on the grounds that it will be designed and sailed by people who live at Bondi.

INTERVIEWER Of course, the yachts will be very prominent?

ALAN Extremely prominent, on all the tea-towels spoons, car-seat covers and beach balls.

INTERVIEWER And just finally, commodore, who's going to win the big race?

ALAN Oh, well that's difficult to say – it's still under negotiation. . .

AMERICA'S CUP ENDING

It is perhaps a pity that with such extensive preparations the yacht club forgot one thing – a faster boat. As a special tribute to their efforts, Westpac presented the Kookaburra Syndicate with a Gold Spanner – to hit Iain Murray over the head with.

INSTITUTE OF SPORT

IOS Canberra

You know, Australia has always had a marvellous sporting reputation. Just look at some of our great runners; Herb Elliot, Betty Cuthbert, Robert Trimbole - to name the fastest. Even now at the Institute of Sport in Canberra, we're training our athletes to new levels of fitness, discipline and oral hygeine, and stitching them into tighter Speedos than ever before.

In 1988, these young men and women, the thickened cream of Australia's sporting talent will be boarding a plane for Seoul. And by the time they're carried off at the other end, and the toilets have been hosed out, the Olympic Games will be on again. Then all that stands between Australia and Gold, will be the three big "F"s Fearlessness, Fortitude, and luck,

I wish it for you all,

Director, IOS

SPORTSMEN THRU' THE AGES

'It was nice to get the triple century, but I must say it was a beautiful batting wicket.'
Don Bradman (1933)

'Oh, the crowd were fantastic, I owe it all to them, it was great to win the gold medal for the crowd's sake.'
Herb Elliot (1957)

'It was an honour to be in the pool with such marvellous swimmers. It was nice to win today, but everything did go right for me.'
Dawn Fraser (1960)

'I was very lucky to win. John was extremely worn out by the match last night. I'd like to thank the organisers who are . . .
Rod Laver (1968)

'. . . the biggest bunch of pricks I have ever had the misfortune to come across. How am I expected to win if . . . and you can print this . . . if I don't get any back-up from the officials? I've been carrying an injury for two months, but do I get any support from the sports federation or the government . . .'
anyone (1987)

91

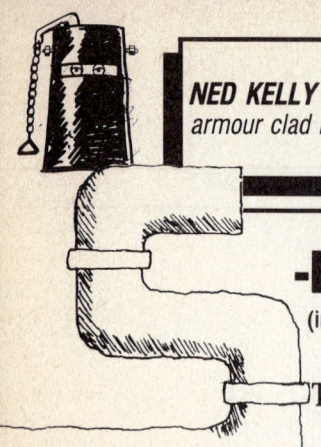

-BEND ACTION

(inc. AUSTRALIAN PLUMBING MONTHLY)

The Magazine by, and for, the Brown Collar Worker

Featuring;

* Blockage of the week p3
* Odours-a new perspective p5
* The Triple-F Back-wash Valve – we take it on a test run after breakfast p12
* PLUS!!!!
  This week's letters

Dear S-B,
I've been using the Winsom Double J4 fitting, since I began bathroom renovations two years ago. However, some friends told me the Polythene WW5's are more resistant to corrosion. Is this true?

John M (WA)

Dear John,
A lot of men are troubled by the size of their penis. However, let me assure you that surveys have shown conclusively that size is not important for women. So quit worrying, and get on with plumbing.

Dear S-B,
Have porcelain bowls definitely had their day? Or will the advent of larger cisterns see a decline in the enamel treated bowl surface?

Arthur J (NSW)

Dear Arthur,
I assure you that women can still achieve orgasm with a small penis. Really. Please believe me! Penis size is NOT worth worrying about!

Dear S-B,
I've been reading your letters column over the past few years. Do you have a complex about the size of your penis?

Simon J (Qld)

Dear Simon,
The SL 8 mains pressure cycle indicator is considered by master-tradesmen to be far inferior to the flow-cycle filters manufactured over the past few years.

A TURD FROM OUR EDITOR

G'day, fellas. One of the great aspects of my job is that in selecting features for 'Action', I get to read thousands of words about other plumbers' lives. The doings of these people are fascinating, although there are some who've had so much publicity we tend to groan every time we see their faces (that's right, I said faces)

I felt that way when the feature of Ralph Dobson (pages 8-11) arrived on my desk – until I started reading it. It's one of the best interviews ever recorded with this amazing drainage expert that I can remember. I hope you enjoy it, too.

There are lots of other interesting tradesmen in our 'People in Focus' lift-out, such as Frank Caperelli, who seems to have got over his son's tragic TR-4 Ball-cock habit; the amazing Ted Calwell, the man who put the 'C' into septic tank; Alf Williams, writing on his battle against blockage; and exclusive pictures of Alex Dimitriou's new work van (including the aluminium ladder on top that everyone's talking about).

And find out if you have what it takes to make an impact on the septic scene with our 'Sewerage Aptitude Quiz'.

Famous plumbers are envied by some . . . but would you want to be famous? Make the final decision after you've read our 'Good Toilet' article on the therapeutic effect of bathing in fresh sewerage by associate editor, Reg 'Stinky' Mullane. Personally, I'd prefer the anonymity of the bathroom fittings warehouse.

Until next week . . .

Cyril Perkins
Editor

DRAMA IN REAL LIFE!

TRAPPED! In another predictable location.

Friday, 22 June; the end of another working week. I had just closed up my office on the 3rd floor. (I'm 2IC in a successful insurance brokerage) and headed towards the lift. It would be good to get home. My girlfriend had a big evening planned for us, a baked dinner, and then later – we were going to put up shelves. The lift wasn't too crowded, I noted, as I got in, careful not to invade anyone's personal space (Little things like that are important in the insurance industry.) Suddenly! Disaster struck!

SUDDENLY DISASTER STRUCK

The lift jerked to a halt and the lights flickered. It was then that I realised, we were trapped, midway between the first and second floors!

LUCKILY, I USED TO FLY CHOPPERS IN 'NAM

Luckily, I used to fly choppers in 'Nam, but even so, this lift panel was pretty new to me. Just a lot of buttons and flashing lights. The flood waters were rising fast, and I knew that if we didn't get out of here soon, before the air pocket ran out and the glacier slipped, our chances would be pretty slim. The girl from accounts had twisted her

THE CONTRACTIONS WERE COMING EVERY TWO MINUTES

ankle moving to the back of the lift and needed medical help fast. What's more, the contractions were coming every two minutes now, and two or three from typing pool were starting to lose their cool. Two minutes! Don't panic! I told myself, grabbing an old hunting rifle (that belonged to my grandfather) down from over the fire. But which button to press? The wrong choice could send us hurtling towards the basement. Sweat poured from my brow and bulging pectorals. Another hour and it would be too late. 'Skip, take a message to Sonny,' I shouted. Just then I knew exactly what had been causing the tremors . . .
(cont p157)

ERROL FLYNN *One of Tasmania's greatest sons, this swashbuckling superstar of the silver screen never let fame go to his head. It did, however, affect other parts of his anatomy and he died of gonorrhoea.*

CHEZ JOE'S

24 hour A La Carte Bistro and
Roadside Cafe

◆

ONTRAY:
*SOUP DE TOMATO
(Delicately opened tin of
condensed soup, heated slowly for
twelve hours with just a hint of last
week's mixed vegies we couldn't
scrape off the pot)

*OYSTERS KILL PATRICK
(Cooked Yabby)

*Lambs Fry
(Sheeps' Balls)

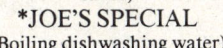

◆

MAIN COARSE:
*CHOPS ET SNAGS
(Selected tender cuts of fine beef
charred beyond recognition and
served on a delicate bed of tomato
sauce)

*JOE'S SPECIAL
(Boiling dishwashing water)

◆ OR ◆

TRY OUR FIXED
PRICE TRUCKIE
MENU

Pie	(with sauce)
Pastie	(with sauce)
Bucket of Chips	(with sauce)
Sauce	(with sauce)
Pckt of Cigs	(with sauce vinegar)

$5.00

◆

CHEZ JOE'S
– on the Hume Hwy, just over the
Vic. Border.
– Weddings catered for.
– party bookings for anything up to
8 wheels

Here's what the *GOOD
FOOD GUIDE* said about us:
'Chez Joe's has all the bucolic
charm one would expect from a
dose of dysentry.'
– PRETTY BIG WORDS, EH?

BOOK NOW!

95

BIRTH, CONTROL OF

In a recent survey taken amongst Catholic women, we discovered that almost half were regularly using some form of birth control. Now, that's quite alarming, especially when you consider the number of nuns we spoke to, and so it seemed high time to go through the basic rules from a Catholic point of view.

The most common form of birth control today is the pill. Also known as the contraceptive pill, the oral contraceptive for women, and 'what pills, mum? they're vitamin C tablets.' The pill is right out for us Catholics, as are rubber devices, plastic implants and IUDs (except after 9 pm, when it's cheaper to phone).

However, the Church does offer many alternative methods of birth control. The most pouplar is, of course, guilt; followed by fear, ignorance and the threat of lasting visual impairment. But the safest form of contraception amongst Australian women is, without doubt, the velour dressing gown. This method provides almost 100 per cent protection against the risk of pregnancy, especially when used in conjunction with an approved pair of fluffy slippers.

Dear Alf,
I counted six Asians on the train today, and two near the RSL last night. You wouldn't read about it. If things keep going this way, they'll be taking our jobs. Lucky we're both unemployed. Still, they come out in their bloody gondolas and start amassing their fortunes. And you know why don't you Alf, because they work harder than us, the cheeky beggars.
    And you know they're taking our children's places at the university. My boy swears he didn't get into Uni because one of them slanty eyes took his place. Also because he failed Form 3; still, you wouldn't read about it would you? I saw in the paper that they actually BBQ their dogs. Thank God we drowned ours when they were pups. You wouldn't read about it.

                    Your Mate Perc.
PS: Get one of the nurses to read this to you.

'What I like about Australia is that you can be sexist and racist and it doesn't affect your social life.'

INSTRUCTIONS FOR BRITISH OFFICER-IN-CHARGE: MARALINGA

1/ Have all preliminary checks been completed? ☑

2/ Has all the civilian population been cleared from the test site? ☑

3/ Has the Aboriginal population been cleared from the test site? ☐

4/ Have all devices been detonated? ☑

After completion of tests, evacuate British Military and scientific personal asap. If you encounter any problems from the locals (and that chap with the bushy eyebrows from Canberra seems to have them pretty well duped), simply explain that Britain is their Ally and that She would never compromise Australia's interests to further her own. They should fall for this line. It seemed to work at Gallipoli, and they have been impressed with it ever since.

Neckwear around the world

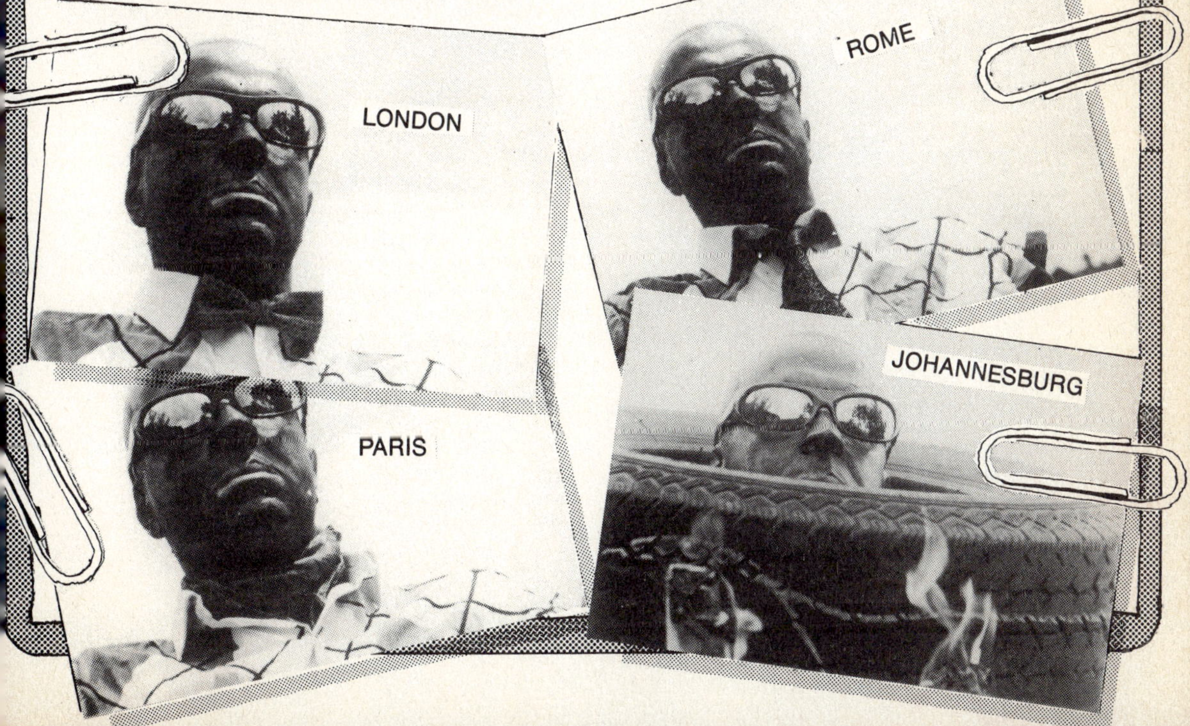

LONDON

PARIS

ROME

JOHANNESBURG